The Universe of Faiths

*A Critical Study of John Hick's
Religious Pluralism*

Christopher Sinkinson

paternoster press

Paternoster Press is an imprint of Paternoster Publishing,
P.O. Box 300, Carlisle, Cumbria, CA3 0QS, UK
and
P.O. Box 1047, Waynesboro, GA 30830-2047, USA
Website: www.paternoster-publishing.com

British Library Cataloguing in Publication Data
A catalogue record for this book is available from the British Library

ISBN 1-84227-106-7

Cover Design by FourNineZero
Typeset by WestKey Ltd, Falmouth, Cornwall
Printed in Great Britain by Bell & Bain, Glasgow

Contents

Foreword

The question of the relationship between Christianity and non-Christian religions is one of the most pressing theological questions of our time. Perhaps no one has written as clearly or as profusely on the subject as the Christian theologian/philosopher, Professor John Hick, and his influence is widespread. Hick has advanced a new approach to the world religions which, roughly speaking, views all the major religions as more or less equal paths to the divine. Clearly, he is controversial and his view deserves serious attention. Much attention has been paid to Hick's Christology and his doctrine of the divine reality. Chris Sinkinson's new book is one of the most thorough and perceptive critical examinations of the influential work of John Hick that I have read. Sinkinson offers a fair and balanced exposition of Hick's position before subjecting it to searching biblical, theological, philosophical and historical questions. Sinkinson's study makes a major advance in both the study of John Hick and more generally, in the field of theology of religions by his penetrating epistemological attention to Hick's presuppositions.

In Chapters One and Two Sinkinson surveys the development of Hick's position through a brief biographical reflection on his life. His major writings are summarised with reference to developments in his own academic career. Having briefly described the position that has come to be known as 'Religious Pluralism' Sinkinson then set out to explore its coherence and its implications. One of his primary and novel arguments is that Hick's position is even more coherent than some of his critics allow. Far from being a revolution in his thought, the religious pluralist position is simply the logical outcome of Hick's earliest ideas.

In order to establish this Chapter Three involves a detailed exposition of Hick's epistemology as it was stated before his interest in theology of religions, before his Copernican Revolution. In Chapter Four Sinkinson discusses his epistemology as presented in his later work. In a fundamental way Hick's theory of knowledge has never really changed. He has always been committed to a position not unlike that of the Sceptic tradition in philosophy. According to this school of thought there can never be certainty in matters of fundamental importance. Sinkinson is quite unique in locating Hick in this tradition and his epistemological placing of Hick is enormously helpful.

In Chapters Five and Six Sinkinson pursues this attempt to place Hick in his philosophical context by assessing the relationship between his work and that of the great German philosopher Immanuel Kant. Far from being of marginal significance Sinkinson proposes that Hick is profoundly indebted to the theological project of which Kant was a part. For that reason, the problems associated with the work of Kant may also be redirected at the work of Hick.

The implications of such a modernist project are explored in chapters Seven and Eight where Sinkinson tries to demonstrate the impoverished view of religion underlying Hick's theology. His emphasis on personal experience, universal feelings and individualism serves to flatten the genuine diversity of the world religions.

Sinkinson takes these criticisms further in Chapter Nine where he point out that if one adopts Hick's position on the world religions then one is committed to a theology devoid of the possibility of revelation. It is not simply that 'God' or the 'Real' has chosen not to communicate, but the Divine Being is absolutely unable to do so. The absence of a doctrine of revelation undermines any attempt to interpret Hick as a Christian philosopher or theologian. In the last analysis his work is not really about 'God' at all, but about the experience of humankind. Religious pluralism is not really an 'interpretation of religion' but an exposition of an alternative religion not unlike deism. Sinkinson's criticisms are perceptive and very thoughtfully developed - and in my view, entirely apposite. We shall be indebted to his critique and I am sure it will be much discussed.

In the final chapter Sinkinson ties together these criticisms of Hick with suggestions as to the development of an alternative account of religious pluralism. In particular, Sinkinson suggests that religious pluralism destroys diversity in favour of presenting a harmonious reading of the religions. Instead, Sinkinson points out that genuine tolerance and humility demand that we acknowledge our differences and disagreements in order to live peacefully in disharmony. Whether such a peace is possible may be questionable but the alternative proposed by Hick is not really the reconciliation of religions but their redundancy. Those who adhere to the pluralist framework base their religious tolerance on an unspoken agreement to dispense with any belief that might cause offence. This chapter leaves us hungry to see how Sinkinson will develop his own position in later publications and shows that he is entirely capable of both critical and constructive theology.

Readers will enjoy Sinkinson's lucid, rigorous, and challenging style, and whether they agree with his conclusions or not, they will have to rethink many issues regarding Christianity and other religions in the light of this book. Along with his epistemological investigations, this book establishes Sinkinson as one of the new bright lights of British theology.

Gavin D'Costa
Reader in Christian Theology
University of Bristol
June, 2001

Chapter 1

Evangelical to Radical

Introduction

It would be a thoughtless Christian who did not at some stage feel the challenge of the world religions in the contemporary age. Whether being taught religious education at school, studying alongside friends from many cultures at university or having work colleagues from different traditions, our encounter with religious diversity is unrelenting. What is the Christian to make of this diversity? Are all other religions false? Are the adherents of other religions facing an eternal death? Or do religions vary in their validity and usefulness? Perhaps all, or most, religions share in a common divine significance?

The twentieth century has witnessed great cultural and philosophical upheaval in the western world, but the predicted demise of religious belief has failed to materialise. In fact, there has been great growth in religious diversity. The only plausible demise on the horizon seems to be that of secular atheism. According to a recent survey a mere 4.4 per cent of Europeans claim to be atheist.[1] The real change has been to an awareness of many religious options and to subtle alterations in religious self-understanding. Christians, along with adherents of other faiths, have become less dogmatic regarding the truthfulness of their own religious persuasion. While Christianity has not died it has undergone radical re-evaluation. It is no exaggeration to say that what will be described as 'Christian' theologies in the twenty-first century

---

[1] The European Values Study 1996. Cited in Ramachandra, *Faiths in Conflict?*, 142.

would have been unrecognisable as Christian at the beginning of the twentieth century.

In order to understand these changes and to evaluate new definitions of Christian thought, we shall explore, in detail, the position of one particular thinker. The reason for focusing on a single theologian is not difficult to justify. John Hick has spanned much of the twentieth century and had to grapple first hand with philosophical and cultural developments in the contemporary age. In some senses his own life encapsulates those changes as he has moved from a position of Christian orthodoxy to one that many Christians would consider heretical. His writing is crystal clear, sometimes polemical, and has been highly influential. No academic study of the Christian response to religious diversity is complete without interaction with his work; and no academic religious studies course has truly equipped its students unless they are familiar with his arguments.

However, our interest in this detailed focus is more than simply in order to describe the developments in his theological thought. We shall also be able to trace the influences on western thought that have led to this position being tenable and find major fault lines in this work. Establishing those faults will allow us to re-evaluate the contemporary responses to religious diversity and ask whether there might not be a better way.

The first two chapters will be largely concerned with a descriptive account of Hick's journey to a radical new theology. Chapters 3 and 4 will unpack the philosophical foundations for this theology. Then in Chapters 5 and 6 we shall be able to embark on an archaeological dig. Our aim will be to find the historical precedent for the new theology in order to aid our assessment of it. Only in Chapters 7 to 10 do we critique and, finally, reject this approach to diversity.

Journey to Faith

John Harwood Hick was born on 20 January 1922 in Scarborough, Yorkshire. His childhood was not marked by any great interest in religion, as he found the parish church his family attended a matter of 'infinite boredom'.[2] He did meet George Jeffreys, one of the

---

[2] Hick, *God Has Many Names*, 1.

founding figures of the Elim Pentecostal Church, in the 1930s. Jeffreys was visiting the home of Hick's grandmother when Hick was a child and, joining in a prayer meeting, Hick 'felt a strong physical effect, like an electric shock except that it was not a sharp jolt but a pervasive sensation spreading down through my body'.[3] The experience left Hick with an intense feeling of emotional release. Nonetheless, he remained unimpressed with Christianity and felt some attraction to a western form of Hindu philosophy known as Theosophy.

Hick initially read law at Hull University and during the first year 'underwent a spiritual conversion' and 'became a Christian of a strongly evangelical and indeed fundamentalist kind'.[4] His conversion brought him into contact with the Inter-Varsity Fellowship Christian Union and, through this movement, identification with what he describes as 'Calvinist orthodoxy of an extremely conservative kind'.[5] Hick had come to believe in the inerrancy of Scripture, the virgin birth and the literal incarnation of Christ, but all these beliefs would later be modified or dropped.

Hick's interest in religion was now awakened and in 1940 he began to study philosophy at Edinburgh University. It was here that his disillusionment with evangelicalism began. The war interrupted his studies and, as a conscientious objector, Hick served with the Friends Ambulance Unit. Consequently, he did not graduate from Edinburgh until 1948, when he achieved a first class degree in philosophy. Hick did not rejoin the Christian Union as he began to believe that it was too rigid and narrow-minded in its outlook. For example, he felt that some members were intellectually dishonest in their attempts to reconcile the opening chapters of Genesis with contemporary scientific thought.

He went on to complete a doctorate at Oriel College, Oxford, under the supervision of H.H. Price. The area of his research lay in the philosophy of religion and, in particular, the nature of religious faith. His thesis was later adapted and published as his first book. However, in the immediate future his career did not lie in academia but with the church. After completion of his thesis Hick trained for

---

[3] Hick, *The Fifth Dimension*, 161.
[4] Hick, *Many Names*, 2.
[5] Hick, *Disputed Questions*, 139.

ordination into the English Presbyterian Church. His first pastoral ministry, from 1953 to 1956, was at Belford Presbyterian Church. During this time he married Hazel Bowers.

At this stage in Hick's life he still considered himself to be a conservative Christian. Although he was greatly frustrated with evangelicalism he would still have affirmed many of the historic doctrines of the Christian church. His frustration lay in what he perceived as intellectual weaknesses among evangelicals who, in particular, did not seem to engage critically with difficult issues.

Hick was more a philosopher than a theologian, as philosophy had been his main area of study. Though his Presbyterian training included the study of theology at Westminster College, Cambridge, his formal degrees were in philosophy – his doctorate in theology was an honorary degree from Uppsala University in Sweden. Hick's philosophical training explains why much of his work was devoted to exploring the foundations of Christian thought and belief. It is to this philosophical work that much of the argument of this book will be devoted.

Philosophical Work

In 1956 Hick was appointed Assistant Professor of Philosophy at Cornell University and so began his academic career. During this time he developed his doctoral thesis and published it as the book *Faith and Knowledge*. This book has been reprinted many times and remains a very popular account of Christian epistemology. As we shall later see, its basic arguments remain Hick's consistent position throughout his work. Though his beliefs would undergo major modification, his basic epistemology would not.

Epistemology deals with the theory of how we know anything at all. The epistemology of religion raises all kinds of interesting questions, as the beliefs of religious people can be both highly contentious and deeply profound. Hick uses the term 'faith' to describe religious knowledge. He rejects a model of faith that he describes as 'Thomist-Catholic', after the theologian Thomas Aquinas. According to this model, faith is a matter of assenting to the truth of certain beliefs, including the Trinity, the incarnation, and so forth. In contrast, Hick proposes a model of faith that is to do with subjective, personal experience rather than with intellectual abstraction. Our experience leads us to interpret the world around us in the way we do; and faith is this act of interpretation applied to the religious dimension of existence. It is not a response to verbal, doctrinal statements but to the religious significance of the world. Hick argues for this position by showing how all knowledge, religious and otherwise, follows this same pattern: all knowledge is the human interpretation of objective realities.

There are four levels or types of interpretation. The first is that of *natural knowledge*. At this level there is the least ambiguity in what we see and, correspondingly, the greatest extent of agreement among people on how we should interpret things. Even if someone were not sure what a lamp-post might be they would probably still interpret it as a hard, perpendicular object and walk around it rather than into it.

The second level is that of *moral judgement*. Situations inviting a moral response offer a greater degree of subjective freedom. For example, the Nazi leadership of Germany probably exercised their moral judgement differently than most people would in their situation. Thus, despite anomalies, there is a high degree of moral agreement around the planet on issues like murder, theft and deception.

The third level is that of *aesthetic taste*, which allows greater freedom still. Our interpretation of the artistic value of something we see, hear or read depends upon many subjective factors. Consequently, there is much less agreement among people on what should be judged as good or bad art.

The final level of knowledge is *religious faith*. The difference between this level of belief and those previous levels lies in the fact that religious faith involves a total interpretation of the universe. Faith is not the interpretation of just one aspect of reality, but involves our relationship to reality as a whole. In itself the universe is ambiguous, for although atheists interpret it as devoid of transcendental significance, a convinced believer is able to interpret it as having religious significance. Both believer and non-believer may remain rational in holding alternative beliefs: though at least one or the other must be wrong, it is possible to be both rational and mistaken. Christian faith is a form of religious faith according to which 'in the historical figure of Jesus Christ . . . God has in a unique and final way disclosed himself to men'.[6] Faith is justified by the personal experience of believers, for the universe 'seems' that way to them.

This description of faith, however, might seem to play into the hands of the anti-religious. For example, a movement earlier in the twentieth century, logical positivism, claimed that for language to be meaningful it must make claims that are testable by some form of induction or deduction. Indeed, the meaning of a claim could only be understood in terms of the conditions necessary for its truth value to be tested. Statements that are tautological ('all bachelors are unmarried men') or to do with mathematics ('7 + 6 = 13') can be tested in fairly straightforward ways. But claims regarding physical reality must also be testable. A.J. Ayer offered the principle of verification as a way of distinguishing between intelligible and nonsensical claims.[7] The claim 'all swans are white' is intelligible (even though false) because one could suggest what kinds of tests would be necessary in order to arrive at a verification of the claim. However, the claim 'the entire universe is doubling in size every minute' is meaningless because there would be no way of testing the claim (any instruments of measurement doubling in size along with the universe). The logical positivists used this principle of verification to dismiss metaphysics and religious language. Such language is neither true nor false, argued Ayer, but merely an expression of how someone feels. The principle was subjected to heavy criticism and revision through which a weaker but more influential principle of falsification was devised.

Despite the many problems inherent in the principle of verification, Hick felt its force and sought to respond to it. After all, his own epistemology might suggest that religious language merely expresses how we feel about the universe and says nothing factual about ultimate purpose, God, or life after death. Hick accepted the principle of verification and sought to show how Christianity is verifiable. But the principle of verification does not establish whether a truth claim is true or not; it merely provides the parameters for a test. Once such parameters are established it is clear whether or not the statement really is a meaningful truth claim.

---

[6] Hick, *Faith and Knowledge*, 216.
[7] Ayer, *Language, Truth and Logic*.

Thus, in order to establish that religious claims are genuine truth claims, Hick set himself the task of isolating at least one claim that will be verified by a human subject through sensory experience.

Hick's resolution is known as *eschatological verification*. After all, expectations concerning the future clearly will be confirmed or disconfirmed at some point in the future. For example, if I bet on a horse winning the Grand National there is an obvious future event that will either confirm or disconfirm my prediction. Hick identified such a claim in the Christian language of the afterlife and a future state of bliss, language referring to events that will happen in the future. Hick described the way this principle works in a parable.[8] Imagine two travellers walking along the same road, but who hold different opinions about where the road leads. One believes it leads to a celestial city, whereas the other believes it leads nowhere. As the road itself remains ambiguous, providing no conclusive evidence either way, both travellers must be content to recognise that their beliefs about the destination of the road are matters of opinion. However, their division of opinion is over a matter of fact, and one event in the future would verify the claim of the celestial-city believer: in the event of rounding a corner and arriving at the city, his or her belief would be proven true. The parable shows how a real truth claim is at stake and that a real situation is possible, which would confirm that claim.

Analogously, a post-mortem encounter with God would be a real, sensory experience that would verify the Christian claim. On dying and entering a world beyond the grave the Christian claims would be verified. Because such an eventuality is always possible, Christian claims regarding life after death are meaningful truth claims. But this test is asymmetrical: if there is no afterlife, then nobody will be around to disprove the claim. However, as the principle of verification only requires positive circumstances only in which a claim might be verified, Hick's argument satisfies this demand.

Hick's epistemology has much to commend it. In certain respects he shares in the tradition of Reformed epistemology, which emphasises the self-justifying nature of faith, its personal-subjective quality, and its significance as a worldview. Notable

---

[8] Hick, *Faith*, 177–8.

proponents of this epistemology include Alvin Plantinga and Nicholas Wolterstorff.[9]

The Problem of Evil

Hick moved to Princeton Theological Seminary in 1959 and soon
after this an important controversy flared up. He wished to transfer
his ministerial credentials from the English to the American Presbyterian Church and this provoked a dispute among Presbyterians.
Technically, Hick's position at Princeton and in the Presbyterian
Church assumed adherence to the 1647 Westminster Confession of
Faith. When questioned about his position on the Confession he
expressed doubts over 'the six-day creation of the world, the predestination of many to eternal hell, the verbal inspiration of the
Bible and the virgin birth of Jesus'.[10] His liberal stance, particularly
on the virgin birth, led to a number of Church leaders preventing
the transferral of his ministerial membership. The dispute was then
settled at a national level with a synod ruling in his favour, but
Hick's departure from evangelicalism was now clear. He was not
yet a radical, although there were plenty of radical theological proposals on offer during the 1960s. Rather, Hick was a fairly typical
liberal – denying the historicity of the virgin birth, but still affirming
an orthodox view of the incarnation of Christ.

   Hick returned to England in 1963 and lectured at Cambridge
University. During this time he published his second major work,
Evil and the God of Love. This has also been reprinted many times and
some would hold it to be his best work. The book involves a sustained treatment of various Christian attempts to reconcile the
existence of a good God with the reality of evil and suffering in the
world. Hick compares two alternative traditions in a problem that
has occupied many theologians in church history. He rejects
Augustinian theodicy with its emphasis on divine predestination
and human sinfulness in favour of a modified form of the Irenaean
view. Irenaeus (AD 130–202) described the human struggle against

---

[9] See, e.g., Plantinga and Wolterstorff (eds.), *Faith and Rationality*.
[10] Hick, *Problems of Religious Pluralism*, 2.

evil and suffering as part of the process of developing the divine nature of men and women. According to this model, the 'fall' in the Garden of Eden, recorded in the book of Genesis, was a necessary step towards God rather than a catastrophic falling out of favour with him: it was necessary for Adam and Eve to recognise their weakness, finitude and imperfection. In leaving Eden they began a process of learning morality, love and courage through life in a world of pain. God's creative work involves the permission of evil and suffering in order to prompt the necessary growth in men and women towards an increasing likeness to God. Ultimately, suffering will have been justified because it will have served its purpose in helping humanity towards a higher, noble, goal.

In 1967 Hick took up the H.G. Wood Professorship at Birmingham University and began a phase that would lead to a revolution in his thinking. The most powerful challenge to his theology came not from academic circles but from the city of Birmingham itself. Birmingham had then, as it does now, a large multifaith community including substantial numbers of Muslims, Sikhs and Hindus along with the well-established Jewish community. Hick became aware of the other major world religions in a way that he had not been before. This awareness came largely as a result of his involvement with an inter-religious movement set up in Birmingham to counter racism and in particular the ugly prejudice of the National Front. Hick worked alongside those of other faiths and in so doing was challenged by the quality of life and spirituality that they embodied. He writes, 'Thus it was not so much new thoughts as new experiences that drew me, as a philosopher, into the issues of religious pluralism, and as a Christian into inter-faith dialogue.'[11] These new experiences led to a significant shift in his thinking. Hick had already come to believe in universalism and had felt that adherents of other religions exemplified qualities sometimes missing among fellow Christians. The question then arose: how can only one religion be true?

In 1970 Hick began work on a major book that would mark a departure from his previous studies. This would be an attempt to explore conceptions of the future and the afterlife. However, it would not discuss such profound ideas in isolation from the

---

[11] Hick, *Questions*, 141.

thinking of the various world religions. The eschatology of *Death and Eternal Life*, which we shall consider in more detail later, relates ideas from Christianity to those found in Hinduism and Buddhism. Furthermore, Hick was at this time writing a number of shorter articles arguing the possibility that Christianity was not the one true religion, nor even necessarily a religion superior to any other. He was about to undergo a revolution in his thought, though in order to do so one key Christian doctrine would have to be subjected to substantial modification.

The Copernican Revolution

The major shift in Hick's position was most clearly established in his collection of essays *God and the Universe of Faiths* published in 1973. Three of the essays were originally a series of lectures given at Birmingham University in 1972 and forming a single argument. The titles given to the printed lectures were 'The Essence of Christianity', 'The Copernican Revolution in Theology' and 'The New Map of the Universe of Faiths'. They form a simple and yet powerful argument for what is now known as the *pluralist hypothesis*. Though this hypothesis would be heavily revised in the light of his later thought, its early statement is worth reconsidering here.

By the 'essence' of the Christian faith Hick wanted to identify what mattered most to religious believers. His stated aim was to identify such a matter of importance so that he might then present an inter-religious comparison of what matters most to religious people of various traditions. However, his stipulation regarding what would count as the most important thing is very revealing: 'It is this that we want to compare with the essence of other faiths, rather than any historical peculiarities of the Christian tradition which lie away from its religious centre.'[12]

Notice that Hick assumes in advance that the essence of Christianity cannot be something particular to Christianity – for that would make comparison impossible. Therefore, 'essence' must be something universal, and that will permit the comparison to go ahead. Hick rules out such particularities as the incarnation,

---

[12] Hick, *God and the Universe of Faiths*, 108.

atonement or resurrection from being the essence of Christianity simply because they are not comparable. In effect, Hick is arguing that whatever will facilitate inter-religious comparison must determine how one goes about identifying the essence of Christianity. Whatever is unique, special or contingent to a historical context must 'lie away from', in Hick's words, the essence of faith. Ruled out, a priori, in his method is the possibility that what might matter most to religious people, or be of the essence of their faith, is a historical event or a unique person.

What does Hick propose to be the essence of Christianity? He traces the New Testament description of salvation as a 'way' and concludes that the essence lies not in right belief but in right behaviour. Salvation is not about coming to hold certain doctrines as true but about living life in a certain way. According to Hick, what is distinctive in the Christian approach to this way is the fact that it is tied to a particular historical figure: 'The life, death and resurrection of Jesus of Nazareth, his influence upon those who responded to him in faith, their memories of him and of his words, and their experiences of a new quality of life in a new relationship with God and with one another'.[13]

The essence of Christianity is, then, a practical way of living inspired by the Christ event. However, this seems inconsistent with his methodological commitment to finding an essence that is not related to any historical particularities. For this reason, Hick denies that the Christ event is an event in public history, preferring to see it as an event experienced in faith. Indeed, Hick is convinced that the actual history of Jesus is now beyond recovery by normal methods of research. Therefore, the essence of Christianity is a way of life inspired by some form of experience of the Christ image. This rather less specific focus fits well with his desired aim to identify an essence that does not rely on historical particularities. To be a Christian today is to have an experience inspired by certain images, rather than being a deliberate response to the historic claims of a specific, unique individual called Jesus of Nazareth.

Hick's formulation of the essence of Christianity is really an attempt to continue the classic liberal project of disentangling the Christ of faith from the Jesus of history. He postulates that a process

---

[13] Hick, *God*, 111.

set in very quickly after the death of Jesus whereby the community of people living the new 'way' exaggerated the character of their founder until, within two generations, he was thought of as God. Hick explains this lofty regard for Jesus as simply the way first-century Jews struggled to express their vivid experience in a Judaeo-Greek metaphysical framework. A very different interpretation would have been possible elsewhere: 'In eastern terms he was a *jivanmukti*, or he was a Buddha, one who had attained to true knowledge of and relation to reality.'[14]

The categories in which followers sought to make sense of Jesus were relative to the culture in which they lived. Had the historical Jesus ministered further east, or had the early church been born in the east, then Hick is sure Jesus would have been described in eastern terms and the Christian doctrine of the incarnation would not have got off the ground. It is worth noting here that this discussion of the issues fails to tackle just how radical first-century Christology was. Within the categories of both Hebrew and Greek thought the claims of Christians that Jesus was God incarnate were seen by the pagans as, at best, muddle-headed, and, at worst, blasphemous. Hick's account of the essence of Christianity fails to make sense of the way radical new categories, and even vocabulary, had to be invented in order to describe the identity of Jesus.[15] We shall return to the subject of Christology later.

Having established the essence of Christianity in a particular way of life and quality of experience, Hick continues his comparison of Christianity with other faiths. This leads him, in the second essay, to his famous call for a *Copernican revolution* in theology. Hick is well aware that for much of Christian history the church has sought to maintain an exclusivist stance on the issue of salvation. This is expressed most strikingly in the papal pronouncement *extra ecclesiam nulla salus*, or 'outside the church, no salvation'.[16] Given a quite specific definition of salvation this would be logical. If salvation is

---

[14] Hick, *God*, 115.

[15] Hick's position on the historical Jesus and the Christ event is primarily critiqued in Chapter 10.

[16] For a discussion of the history and significance of this pronouncement see Sullivan, *Salvation Outside the Church?*; and D'Costa, *John Hick's Theology of Religions*, 73–90.

defined as being visibly joined to the historic institution of the church, then the pronouncement is little more than a tautology: outside God's saving work there is no salvation. However, Hick joins many others in expressing his repugnance for such a view of salvation: 'Can we then accept the conclusion that the God of love who seeks to save all mankind had nevertheless ordained that men must be saved in such a way that only a small minority can in fact receive this salvation?'[17]

Hick repeats this question many times in his work, and is aware of attempts to soften these conclusions. There are many theologians who have developed forms of inclusivist theology according to which it is possible for those of other religions to be saved through Christ even though they do not have any specific knowledge of him. Such inclusivist theology has been strong within the Roman Catholic Church since the Second Vatican Council, particularly in the work of Hans Küng and Karl Rahner. Some from an evangelical background have also adopted a form of inclusivist theology.[18] Even conservative evangelicals make exceptions for various categories of people who are physically prevented from expressing explicit faith in Christ. None of these modifications impresses Hick, who draws upon the scientific debate of the sixteenth century to illustrate how the current debate is unfolding and why he will, in the end, be proven right.

Prior to the revolutionary work of Copernicus, Ptolemy had established a picture of the universe that had later been understood as harmonious with the biblical account. According to the Ptolemaic picture, the earth existed at the centre of the universe with the stars, planets and sun revolving around it in concentric circles. However, it was found to be increasingly inaccurate as a way of predicting the positions of the planets. Consequently, astronomers introduced what were known as 'epicycles' to accommodate these irregularities. The planets moved in smaller supplementary cycles during the course of their larger orbit of the earth. With the use of these epicycles, astronomers sought to maintain the Ptolemaic picture of the universe. Tycho Brahe, one of the outstanding observational astronomers of the sixteenth century, suggested such a

---

[17] Hick, *God*, 122.
[18] See, e.g., Pinnock, *A Wideness in God's Mercy*.

revised form of the geocentric system. According to Brahe the sun, the moon and the stars all orbited the fixed earth. The then known five planets orbited the sun, however, that in turn was orbiting the earth. But Brahe's complex system never took on in the astronomical community. A Polish astronomer, Nicholas Copernicus, had already proposed a far simpler and more fruitful model. According to Copernicus, the sun was at rest in the centre of the celestial system and 'epicycles' were no longer necessary to explain the movement of the planets. It was the sun that lay at the centre of the universe, and not the earth.

Hick draws upon this account as an analogy for the development he describes in Christian theology. The older theological picture of salvation as exclusive to the church or to Christianity is considered 'Ptolemaic'. This older picture envisages Christ or the church at the centre of the universe of religions with all others revolving around that centre. The inclusivist strategy of relating religions to Christ through implicit desire for salvation or some similar notion represents the attempt to develop 'epicycles' to account for the problem of plausibility. Karl Rahner, with his inclusivist acccount of Christianity and other religions, would seem to be a kind of theological Tycho Brahe. Hick presents his own position as a revolutionary change in perspective: a theological equivalent to the work of Copernicus.

The Copernican revolution was essentially a change of perspective on our position in the universe. Hick, writing as a Christian theologian, and still not nearly as radical as he would become, calls for such a transformation on the part of the church: 'It involves a shift from the dogma that Christianity is at the centre to the realisation that it is God who is at the centre, and that all the religions of mankind, including our own, serve and revolve around him.'[19]

Of course, the Copernican revolution was not to stop with Christians. Hick also wrote of the need for orthodox believers in all religious traditions to undergo a similar revolution in self-understanding. However, at this stage, Hick was still writing and speaking to a largely Christian audience. Once Christ is seen as other than unique, and certainly not as God, then one can redraw the relationship between Christianity and other faiths.

---

[19] Hick, *God*, 131.

We shall later investigate Hick's Christology in more detail, as this is clearly key to his development. Here, however, let us probe his account of the Copernican revolution a little further. If we grant the accuracy of the analogy, what other implications follow beyond those he expresses?

Using the analogy for theology produces some difficult implications. Julius Lipner pointed out that according to the analogy there are only two positions: the *absolutist* (Ptolemaic) or the *pluralist* (Copernican).[20] The analogy with the Copernican revolution fails at this point because the historical debate concerned two alternatives: either the earth at the centre with complex accounts of planetary motion, or the sun at the centre with a less complex account required. The choice lay between two competing 'exclusivisms'. If the world were populated only by conservative Christians and pluralists then the analogy might be meaningful. However, we live in a world of multireligious diversity where there are many 'exclusivisms'. The analogy with the Copernican revolution breaks down when applied to religious pluralism. Here the choice is between myriad centres of faith, and the problem is why Hick should consider that the choice of 'God' as the centre of faiths is not Ptolemaic, whereas to acknowledge Jesus, Allah, Nirvana or Brahman as the centre is Ptolemaic. Hick's resolution of this problem, at this stage in his career, is to describe the Copernican revolution in theology as the result of one's having to 'stand back in thought from the arena of competing systems, surveying the scene as whole, to see something that is hidden from the Ptolemaic believer'.[21]

What Hick supposes to be hidden from the Ptolemaic believer is the fact that most people tend to follow the religion of their parents and of their culture. Hick claims that if one is able to 'stand back' from personal commitments and loyalties, then one is able to survey all relevant factors as a whole in order to see his basic distinction. The distinction is between the Ptolemaic positions of all mainstream religions and the Copernican shift of perspective in which all of those religions are subjected to one, new, way of thinking. This is not a simple either/or choice between one model and another, as in

---

[20] Lipner, 'Does Copernicus Help? Reflections for a Christian Theology of Religions', 257.
[21] Hick, *God*, 132.

the astronomical analogy, but between loyalty to a religious perspective or a distancing of oneself altogether from such loyalties.

This problem can be pushed further. If the theologies of most
devout people are, in some sense, Ptolemaic (though each claiming
a different centre), then how can Hick maintain that his own position is not also Ptolemaic? After all, does it not claim another
exclusive centre – this time the 'God' beyond Christ? Thus Hick's
Copernican revolution is not really a call to leave exclusivisms
behind, but is a call to entertain a new one, with God at the centre.

The title of the book in which Hick's argument was first published, *God and the Universe of Faiths*, seems a misnomer when
compared with his contemporary position. If 'God' were at the
centre of the universe of faiths then that might satisfy the theistic traditions of Christianity, Judaism and Islam; but what would it have to
say to the agnostic traditions of Hinduism and Buddhism, and to the
atheistic traditions of Zen Buddhism and Shinto?

The Copernican analogy yields another interesting implication
at this point. The change in cosmological perspective did not end
with Copernicus. The sun was at the centre of our own solar system, but the entire universe, including the celestial firmament with
its zodiacal constellations, did not really revolve around the sun.
The centre of the universe would have to shift elsewhere. Indeed, in
later astronomical developments talk of a central pivot seemed less
helpful in relation to the motion of the galaxies. This change is also
evident in Hick's work as later speculation leads him to shift the religious centre away from God to the 'Real'.[22] It is this process that can
now be traced through the further stages of Hick's career. In a sense,
the Copernican revolution set Hick on a trajectory away from God
being at the centre of faiths.

So by 1973 Hick was in print claiming that Christians should not
regard their religion as the one, true way to God but as a single
option among many available in the world today. This also implied
that Christian theology was not the only source of religious truth.
All the religions had potential answers to the ultimate questions of
life and death. For that reason, Hick's work after this time develops
his thought in the context of comparative theology rather than

---

[22] D'Costa, 'John Hick and Religious Pluralism: Yet Another Revolution' in Hewitt (ed.), *Problems in the Philosophy of Religion*, 3–16.

simply Christianity. This significant change in Hick's own work is indicative of a sea change in academic theology, where the emphasis, at least in Britain, would increasingly be on the comparative study of religions.

Chapter 2

The World Religions

John Hick had travelled far in his thinking by the mid 1970s and developed a significant academic reputation in both theology and philosophy. He now had solid credentials to embark on a radical reframing of Christian theology within the context of the world religions. This would lead to further developments in his view of the relationship between Christianity and other religions.

The Afterlife

In 1976 Hick published *Death and Eternal Life*. In this work he does not develop a distinctively Christian approach to the future, but sets out to produce a global theology of the afterlife that interacts with various traditions of thought. He explores ideas about death with reference to existentialist philosophy, parapsychology, humanism and some of the major world religions. Research for his work involved extensive trips to the east including India (1970–71, 1974, 1975–76) and Sri Lanka (1974) during which he developed his understanding of eastern religions. Hick has often drawn on the data provided by parapsychology and accounts of near-death experiences to help bolster his idea that the universe has a religious dimension and that the human person will continue, in some form, beyond the grave. Hick is a 'critical realist' about religious language. This means that while he accepts that some religious language is poetic or 'mythological', there remains a core of literal truth including the claim that existence continues beyond the grave. Hick rejects the concept of hell or eternal punishment in favour of belief in a universal salvation. He is optimistic that all people will enjoy a future existence beyond death that will, eventually, l[...] solute bliss. The resurrection of the body is the mythological [...] given for this in Christian thought.

The world views of eastern religions shed further [...] the conclusions of Hick, who argues that the concept of rei[...]n is compatible with Christianity. However, while eastern [...]ern religions share the belief that existence continues after [...]ey disagree over whether this future life involves a return to this world or a transformation into another state in another world. Hick proposes that the self will progress through many further worlds in which he or she will have further opportunities to achieve the goal of moral and spiritual perfection. Reincarnation and resurrection are taken to be compatible, mythological, ways of describing this process.

The argument of *Death and Eternal Life* requires that there be an ultimate, transcendent significance to the 'self'. But neither the term 'God' nor the western notion of 'self' translates readily into eastern terms. Indeed, many schools of Hinduism and Buddhism deny that there really is a true self and, furthermore, consider the very notion that we are individuals to be one of the very causes of ignorance from which we need to be released. According to these traditions, the ultimate state is not a matter of individuals enjoying the company of a God from whom they are distinct, but lies in the individual being absorbed into the ultimate reality, much as a drop of water might be absorbed into an ocean. Consequently, at this stage in his writing Hick sides with one tradition of Hindu thought against another in retaining belief in the transcendental significance of the self and the ultimate distinction between self and God. Hick must explicitly repudiate one important stream of Hindu thought in order to commit himself to this conclusion – a commitment that would later change: the more radical version of his pluralist hypothesis would require that no one tradition of Hinduism would have supremacy over the other.

The Identity of Jesus Christ

One of Hick's first published articles, in 1948, was a critique of the Christology of D.M. Baillie. Hick criticised Baillie for failing to provide a Christology that fully reflected the historic position of the church represented in the creeds. Hick's basic commitment to an orthodox, creedal, Christology remained during the fifties (though without belief in the virgin birth) but began to be brought into question as he developed his pluralist view of the world religions. His encounter with men and women of other faiths brought his Christology into question. If Jesus was truly the unique incarnation of God on earth, then other religions, at best, are relegated to being temporary movements awaiting fulfilment in Christ or, at worst, human perversions blinding people to the truth of Christ as God's sole means of salvation. The Copernican revolution in theology demanded a revision of Christology.

A new view of Jesus was proposed in *God and the Universe of Faiths*, but this position still entailed a high view of Jesus as incarnating the divine love. Hick entirely abandoned the orthodox view of Christ soon after this, in an infamous 1977 publication, *The Myth of God Incarnate*. He edited this collection of essays which all cast doubt on the possibility that Jesus was God incarnate in any literal sense. The consensus of the contributors seemed to be that Jesus did not understand himself to be God, and that the source of the doctrine lay more in misunderstood Near Eastern mythology and Greek philosophy than in the Bible.

Hick's problem with the doctrine of the incarnation was that it attempted to describe the identity of Jesus as of one substance with God. The notion of 'substance' implied in this claim was tied to a particular Greek thought world and alien both to the Bible and to the modern world. He questioned how it could be possible that one, historical, particular, limited, fallible human could also be the one, eternal, infinite, perfect divine being. For example, if one affirms that Jesus was limited in knowledge (as the gospels describe at certain points: Matt. 24:36; Mark 5:30), then, Hick claimed, he cannot be the same individual as the all-knowing God. Or, if one affirms that Jesus really was omniscient and omnipotent, then he argues that Jesus could not really have been a human being after all. According to Hick, affirming the identity of God and Christ as being of one substance is like affirming the existence of a square circle – it is a contradiction in terms and, therefore, a meaningless claim.

In order to understand Jesus in a way more compatible with his Copernican revolution, Hick described Christology in terms of relationship rather than substance. He first published his exploration of this view in *God and the Universe of Faiths*. There he dismissed the traditional view as a 'static' concept of the identity of Jesus as God. Instead, he proposed a 'dynamic' concept. The incarnation is not a fact about Jesus but a description of an activity both Jesus and God were engaged in. Jesus incarnated the love of God in his actions towards people. His will was so perfectly matched to that of God that it was possible to say that whatever Jesus willed, God willed. For this reason, the disciples felt as if in the very presence of God.

However, even this view of the incarnation held too high a view of Jesus, making it incompatible with the claims of other religions. Could not similar claims be made of the leaders and founders of other religions? Hick's Christology underwent further revision in the following years. He proposed that Jesus was one saintly figure alongside many others including the Buddha, Zarathustra, Isaiah, Muhammad and Guru Nanak. Thus Hick's developed concept of the identity of Jesus dispensed entirely with any claim to uniqueness. In order to do this he had to deal with the fact that biblical literature and church traditions have presented a high view of the metaphysical status of Jesus. Indeed, a great many Christian apologists have argued against conceptions of Jesus that place him as one great saint among many others.

Hick's answer was to propose that the language of incarnation and divinity applied to Jesus was originally intended as what he calls mythological language. Hick urges Christians to strip away what he sees as later developments in order to see the figure behind the myths. By 'myth' Hick does not here mean that the language is entirely false (see Chapter 8 for further elucidation), but that it is an exaggerated, poetic way of describing the person of Jesus. Behind such mythology, Hick describes the real Jesus as 'intensely and overwhelmingly conscious of the reality of God. He was a man of God, living in the unseen presence of God. He was so powerfully God-conscious that his life vibrated, as it were, to the divine life; and as a result his hands could heal the sick'.[1]

---

[1] Hick, *Evil and the God of Love*, 172.

Hick's new Christology dispensed entirely with the unique status of Jesus as God incarnate in favour of Jesus as a man imbued with a sense of God – just as had been the case with other great religious people of the past. The difference between Jesus and ourselves is not an absolute difference but a matter of degree. Jesus incarnated a consciousness of God much more than many of us are capable of.

The Case for Pluralism

The revised Christology allowed the Copernican revolution to develop even more radical conclusions. Most of Hick's printed output after this time concerned the pluralist hypothesis. He refined it further and answered the charges of his critics, which culminated in his most significant work, published in 1989, *An Interpretation of Religion*. Here Hick restated his basic epistemology: all knowledge, religious and otherwise, involves the interpretation of the complex reality around us so that we can make sense of it.

In this work he was able to clarify his thought on epistemology and draw together threads of thought which had been explored since his PhD thesis on faith and knowledge. Using Jastrow's picture of the duck-rabbit, Hick points out how a pattern of lines on paper can be interpreted in two different ways: as a rabbit or as a duck. Borrowing the terminology, if not the philosophy, of Ludwig Wittgenstein (1889–1951) Hick describes this experience as 'seeing-as'.[2] We see the picture 'as' a duck or 'as' a rabbit, the picture in itself being ambiguous, open to either interpretation.

Similarly, suggests Hick, we can experience the world in different ways. For example, before the Mars Observer sent back stunning high-resolution photographs of the Martian surface there were all kinds of odd shapes to be seen in the earlier Viking photographs, including one photo of a rock looking distinctly like that of a face, half in shadow. The later high-resolution photographs revealed this to be a trick of the light and human imagination. It was

---

[2] This important element of his epistemology was developed after the publication of *Faith and Knowledge* and is found in 'Religious Faith as Experiencing-as' in Paul Badham (ed.), *A John Hick Reader*, 34–48. This essay was first published in 1969.

nothing more than a natural rock formation. But the earlier photo-graph does testify to the role of the observer in making sense of the world around. We look for patterns and shapes, and when we see the world in a certain way that makes sense it can be hard to shake our faith in what we believe we have seen. There are videos, books and magazines promoting the idea of an ancient city on Mars, based around the mysterious face formation.

Hick describes the activity of the human mind as more than sim-ply seeing; it is 'experiencing-as'. We experience the world around us in a certain way as we interpret the sights, smells, tastes, sounds and feeling of surfaces around us. As we saw in his first published work, there are four levels of this interpretative activity, the highest of which is the religious or total interpretation. Religious belief attempts to make sense of the whole range of human experience.

But Hick went further than he had done in earlier work in emphasising the organising nature of the mind. Borrowing from the work of Kant, Hick postulated that the Ultimate Reality, the 'noumenon', was beyond any possible human experience. The reality we experience is the 'phenomenon', or the way the 'noumenon' *appears* to us. This Kantian epistemology allowed Hick to make a radical distinction between the descriptions of God offered by the world religions and the Ultimate Reality behind those descriptions. Utterly conflicting truth claims need no longer be a problem. Religions are not offering complete descriptions of God, but only partial descriptions of their own experience of what lies beyond. Even the most different and apparently contradictory descriptions could ultimately be compatible given how unknow-able the Real truly is. In keeping with this epistemology, it would not make sense to speak of 'God' and the 'universe and faiths', as 'God' is a word of description in the realm of phenomenon. A better expression now would be 'Ultimate Reality' and the 'uni-verse of faiths'. Hick proposes the 'Real' or 'Ultimate Reality' as less loaded terms to refer to the divine being than terms like God, Allah or Brahman.

What then of religion? According to *An Interpretation of Religion*, religions are human constructs that provide a context in which we can dimly experience the Ultimate Reality; they are not disclosures of that reality or repositories of revealed truths. Given this frame-work, most of the major world religions can be recognised as of largely equal value in securing this experience. But Hick does not simply dispense with the significance of religious truth claims. Instead, he develops his epistemology of critical realism.

Critical realism is an interpretation of the value of religious language and knowledge. According to naïve realists such language is simply a direct, literal claim about ultimate realities. So when naïve realists describe God as love they mean that God really is a personal being living in heaven and capable of loving relationships. In contrast to naïve realism, during the twentieth century a great deal of theology developed that described itself as 'non-realist'. If non-realists describe God as love, all they mean to affirm is something positive about the qualities of love and its importance for human relationships. To non-realists, therefore, the statement 'Love is God' is the same as 'God is Love.' They do not believe that their language describes a transcendental reality beyond our own existence. Hick offers critical realism as a middle position. He does not accept that the language of religion gives a literal description of the divine being. However, he maintains that language is still 'realist' in the sense that it assumes there really is a transcendent being, however limited and vague our descriptions of it may be.

Hick's most recent major book was published in 1999, under the title *The Fifth Dimension*. Although much of this work is a restatement of his well-established position, he now draws more on the evidence of mystics and has other examples of individuals who have lived in the light of the Ultimate Reality. This evidence, he suggests, points to the possibility that there really is a fifth dimension to our existence, beyond space and time, in which divine reality may be experienced. This book confirms Hick's absolute commitment to the pluralist hypothesis and to his critical realism. He is not suggesting that religions are merely poetic imagery, but remains convinced that there really is some form of continued existence beyond the grave and some form of divine, transcendent reality.

Continuity or Discontinuity?

The corpus of Hick's work, briefly surveyed here, spans forty years. We have noted major shifts in his thinking and how this has been expressed in his writing. Essentially, Hick moved from being an orthodox Christian, becoming a pluralist, radical theologian in the course of his academic career. Because he has produced so much material it is not surprising that there should be changes and modifications to his thought. I want to suggest, however, that Hick's Copernican revolution, even in its later modified forms, is essentially consistent with his early epistemology. Indeed, my thesis is that the seeds of his pluralism were already sown in his theory of knowledge, and I conclude that there has never been a radical change in Hick's theological framework. Certainly, various theological beliefs have undergone revision but these were only ever peripheral to his basic philosophical commitment. As we shall see, the claim that Hick's work can be treated in such a unified way has been the subject of debate.

Hick notes in his preface to the 1966 second edition of *Faith and Knowledge* that despite the revision he has made to his work, the book remains 'an exposition of the view of faith which seemed to me, and still seems to me, most adequate'.[3] In 1988 there was a reissue of the second edition in which Hick wrote a new preface. Here he continues to maintain that the work is foundational to everything else he has written and notes that his subsequent writings 'proceeded in a natural trajectory from the [earlier] epistemology'.[4] The word 'trajectory' is a useful one and indicates the kind of continuity to be found in Hick's work. Of course, he points out that his theological position has changed substantially, but maintains that 'the theology, whether old or new, does not affect the basic epistemological argument'. This important statement reveals the distinction Hick is happy to make between his philosophy and his theology: his philosophy provides foundations that are stable and compatible with a number of different theological positions, while his theology becomes a kind of second-order discourse.

My intention in this book is to fault the philosophical assumptions underlying pluralism. One criticism is the very notion that philosophy can be pursued as an independent study distinct from theology, and I want to show that this does not happen in Hick's work. His philosophical position *determines* his theological position, for philosophy is not a neutral discipline. This is an inevitable

---

[3] Hick, *Faith and Knowledge*, preface to the second edition.
[4] Hick, *Faith*, preface to the reissue of the second edition.

consequence of his desire to be a consistent thinker. However, there are critics who take a different view.

Gerard Loughlin has proved an unrelenting critic of Hick's work and has drawn attention to the major incoherencies that have developed in the course of the years. In particular, he is critical of the notion that Hick's work can be treated as a unified whole. He goes so far as to make the strong criticism that Hick himself is deluded over the coherence of his literary output. Loughlin's argument is worth surveying here as it seems to conflict with the attempt of this book to deal with Hick's work as a unified project.

Macmillan reissued many of Hick's major works in 1988, each with a new preface. This major publishing venture occurred one year prior to the publication of *An Interpretation of Religion*. Consequently, an impression is given that the corpus of Hick's work forms a coherent whole. The use of prefaces compounds this impression by allowing Hick the space to become, in Loughlin's words, 'the narrator of Hick's texts'.[5] By becoming a narrator of his own work he is able to try to harmonise his conflicting arguments into a single system. The role of the narrator is one who can explain away the significance of changes and smooth over contradictions by pointing out the original intentions of mistaken ideas. Loughlin tries to reveal the underlying discontinuity of Hick's work, prefaces notwithstanding, by describing three 'moments' or temporary phases of his thought: *epistemology*, *Christology* and *theodicy*. By surveying how these have been modified we shall be better able to assess the claim that Hick's work cannot be treated as a coherent whole.

Regarding *epistemology*, Loughlin draws attention to Hick's use of eschatological verification and shows how it develops through three stages. In 1957 his use of the term 'kingdom of God' serves to describe the post-mortem encounter with God. In his 1966 preface he identifies the person of Christ with the kingdom of God in order to make his Christian commitments clearer. However, in 1977 he severs the connection between Christ and the post-mortem encounter. From this point on, the afterlife becomes vague in Hick's work and no longer verifies any particular religious claims that are made in this life other than Hick's rather formal claim that

---

[5] Loughlin, 'Prefacing Pluralism: John Hick and the Mastery of Religion', 30.

there will one day be an unambiguous encounter with the divine presence. This kind of movement away from Christian content towards abstract terms prompts D'Costa to describe the version of eschatological verification that appears in *An Interpretation of Religion* as 'minimalist' because it dispenses with 'specific details of eschatological expectations'.[6]

Regarding *Christology*, Loughlin identifies two different accounts of Christ even since the Copernican revolution. On the one hand, there is a functional account of the incarnation in terms of *agapē*, the love of God and the love of Christ being qualitatively one. However, on the other hand, there is a mythological account of all such incarnational language, which is a poetic way of expressing our own feelings about the Christ story. Loughlin suggests that Hick tries to maintain these two accounts alongside each other even though, strictly speaking, the mythological description renders the functional account redundant. As Hick's work progresses he dispenses altogether with a functional account of the incarnation.

Regarding *theodicy* there has been a striking change in Hick's position. Loughlin charts the change from a Christian theodicy, through a theistic theodicy (not a matter of specific faith in Christ, but a more general belief in God) to a theodicy in keeping with the pluralist shift from 'God' to the 'divine reality'. In order to facilitate this shift, Hick reinterprets his earlier work on theodicy in the light of his ideas about mythological language. 'Hick is able to stand back sufficiently far from his own Irenaean theodicy to see that it is also a myth, just like Augustine's theodicy. He is able to apply to his theodicy the mythographical analysis he had formerly applied only to his *agapē* Christology.'[7]

As with his Christology, so with his theodicy, Hick's earlier Christian understanding of these concepts is emptied of substance in favour of them being seen as helpful myths by which we live. Loughlin notes that myth becomes a useful device in Hick's later writing, enabling him to reinterpret his earlier thought in a way that maintains harmony throughout his work. The substance of

---

[6] D'Costa, 'John Hick and Religious Pluralism: Yet Another Revolution', 7. For a detailed response to Hick's eschatology see Mathis, *Against John Hick*.

[7] Loughlin, 'Prefacing Pluralism', 37.

Loughlin's criticism is that Hick fails to recognise how radical a revision has been made. In some way, each major text that Hick writes presents a major revision of what went before. Indeed, Loughlin even suggests that the revision is so great that each text discards everything that went before. If Loughlin's thesis is correct, then this present attempt to treat Hick's work in terms of a consistent epistemology would be flawed. There are two useful responses to Loughlin's charge we may consider here. The first is that given by Hick.

Hick clearly disliked the tone and style of Loughlin's article, suggesting that it explained his own work as 'an extraordinary – even fantastic – literary conspiracy theory'.[8] In response, Hick points out that his prefaces draw attention both to discontinuities and continuities in his own position.

Concerning epistemology, Hick rejects the notion that eschatological verification ever lay at its heart. He maintains that it is useful to establish the meaningfulness of religious language against the criticisms of the logical positivists. It was never intended, as Loughlin suggests, to establish the truth of Christian belief. Concerning Christology, Hick maintains that Loughlin is mistaken to regard his *agapē* account of the incarnation as a reversal of his earlier orthodox position. A reversal did occur, but later, 'somewhere in the late 1970s'[9] when the *agapē* account had largely been abandoned. This reversal could not constitute a contradiction because by this stage Hick was no longer attempting to hold together an orthodox Christology with the later form of the pluralist hypothesis. In this response, Hick barely deals with Loughlin's objections regarding the use of myth, conceding that it is a 'highly elastic concept' but remains 'a coherent and useful notion'.[10]

Hick freely admits the substantial revision of his position with regard to theodicy, a revision that primarily concerns the way he applies his term 'myth' to accounts of the afterlife. In earlier work, major elements of eschatological language were understood to be literal descriptions of what lies beyond the grave. But now, understanding that language to be mythological, Hick admits that 'it

---

[8] Hick, 'A Response to Gerard Loughlin', 57.

[9] Hick, 'Response', 61.

[10] Hick, 'Response', 61–2.

speaks in human terms of that which transcends the scope of our human capabilities'.[11] Hick maintains that this is a legitimate development of his work rather than an inconsistency. However, this response suggests that Loughlin may have a point here. The reissue of *Evil and the God of Love* gives the impression that Hick's theodicy remains fundamentally unchanged, whereas with Hick's developed philosophy of language we should really be aware that the work is set in a new framework. Language describing the afterlife and ultimate blessing is no longer intended to apply literally to what lies beyond the grave.

Philip L. Barnes has made useful observations on the exchange between Loughlin and Hick that will cast further light on the question of continuity and discontinuity in Hick's work. Barnes notes three senses in which the word 'development' may be used: 'drawing out and making explicit what was originally implicit; rejecting what has gone before; or, finally, expanding one's position by the incorporation of new insights, arguments and ideas'.[12]

Hick's theological position develops in all of these ways and yet none of them necessarily implies inconsistency. Barnes disputes Loughlin's contention that there is a clear contrast between an early and a later Hick position. Rather than discontinuity, Barnes argues for a continuity: 'Hick's theology should be interpreted as the increasingly systematic drawing out of his initial starting point rather than being divided into two different and opposing parts.'[13]

Barnes accepts Loughlin's point that eschatological verification has developed in Hick's work, but argues that this is not really central to his epistemology. Rather, the central notion of Hick's epistemology is that of 'experiencing-as'. The term was introduced in the Royal Institute of Philosophy Lecture series in 1967–68 but described faith in a way entirely consistent with the first edition of *Faith and Knowledge*. In each statement of his epistemology there was a rejection of faith as a cognitive response to doctrinal claims in favour of faith as an interpretative category. The range of possible interpretations considered by Hick grows with his pluralist hypothesis, and yet such a range is easily explained by his conviction

---

[11] Hick, 'Response', 62.
[12] Barnes, 'Continuity and Development in John Hick's Theology', 395.
[13] Barnes, 'Continuity', 396.

that the universe is religiously ambiguous. Thus even his most
recent work maintains the same basic epistemology.

Barnes suggests that the main reason why Loughlin denies the
continuity of Hick's work is that he understands Christology as the
key. There is no doubt that Hick's position underwent radical revolution regarding the identity of Christ and he freely admits this
change. But Barnes maintains that epistemology is the key to Hick's
work and that this is not affected by his view of Christ. Loughlin's
objections would probably apply in the case of most Christian
theologians. Given a substantial revision of the doctrine of the
incarnation one would expect a substantial revision in the rest of a
thinkers' theological position. In Hick's case, Barnes points out,
Christology 'was not an integral part of his epistemology of Christian belief'.[14] Changes in his understanding of Christ have no
bearing on his epistemology because his work bears no intrinsic
relation either to Christian theology in general or Christology in
particular. His work does not now, and never has done. Indeed, the
force of this argument seems so overwhelming that it leads me to
suggest that not only is Hick not properly understood as a Christian
theologian, but that he has never been one. Whatever his personal
beliefs or creed may be, structurally, his work is not Christian.
Much of the argument that follows in this book will substantiate this
claim.

Hick's epistemology is the key element in his work: it has
remained consistent and lends coherence to his system of thought.
Thus his philosophy of knowledge necessarily leads to his pluralist
theology.

Loughlin emphasises discontinuity in Hick's position because he
treats Hick as a Christian theologian. Of the three areas he considers, two are distinctively the arena of Christian theology: *Christology*
and *theodicy*. Even Loughlin's treatment of epistemology is essentially a discussion of eschatology – the theological dimension of
Hick's otherwise non-theological account. Loughlin correctly
identifies the radical discontinuity of Hick's theological position
with regard to eschatology, the person of Jesus and the problem of
evil. However, if one accepts with Barnes that Christian theology
has only ever been marginal to his work, then such discontinuity

---

[14] Barnes, 'Continuity', 400.

loses significance. In terms of epistemology, Hick's position remains largely consistent. Hick deliberately avoids rooting his assumptions in any particular confessional or religious framework, and the result is a work of philosophy that attempts to be theologically neutral. So is it right to see Hick as a theologian? Certainly not, if by this we mean a theologian whose work is founded on a biblical, confessional expression of Christianity. His work is founded on a particular philosophy, not on Christian theology. However, I shall retain the word 'theologian' to describe him because I do not accept that philosophy can be theologically neutral – there are religious commitments underlying Hick's position, but my claim will be that they are not *Christian* religious claims. Hick is a theologian, but the 'theos' of which he speaks is something other than the God of Christian theism.

Chapter 3

On Knowing God

We shall now delve deeper into Hick's theory of religious knowledge and consider the relationship between faith and reason. It is
important to notice that Hick considers himself an apologist for theism. He has argued against atheistic naturalism throughout his
career, claiming that there really is a divine being responsible for
religious knowledge and behaviour in the world. In this chapter we
shall attend to the epistemology of *Faith and Knowledge*. As we have
seen, this was written prior to his adoption of a pluralist theology
and yet his theory of knowledge is happily able to accommodate his
later theological revolution. Furthermore, Paul Helm predicted the
direction of Hick's work when, in responding to his early epistemology, he noted that his description of faith 'requires a different
account of religion as well'.[1] Helm's observation proved to be
astute. As Hick's epistemology is the only stable element in his
entire project, if he can be faulted at this point, then the grounds of
his pluralist proposal are fatally weakened too. This is a bold claim
that I shall now attempt to validate by presenting a detailed description of that epistemology.

Thomist-Catholic Faith

Hick rejects what he describes as the Thomist-Catholic propositional model of faith. With reference to Aquinas, Hick describes this
model as holding faith to be something that relates men and women
to propositions rather than to God. Hick considers this a heavily

---

[1] Helm, *The Varieties of Belief*, 154.

intellectual view of religion. Salvation, according to his description of this model, requires that we 'believe explicitly such central articles as the Incarnation and the Trinity' insofar as one is able to understand their cognitive content.[2] The difference between faith and other forms of intellectual knowledge concerns the degree to which the evidence supports the beliefs. Much everyday knowledge is self-evident, whereas faith is not. Nonetheless, faith is just as certain as everyday knowledge because it involves a subjective commitment to the truth of those beliefs. While the evidence may vary, the personal certainty of the believer need not.

The Thomist-Catholic tradition has held a high view of the capabilities of human reason to establish at least some evidential grounds for holding religious beliefs to be true. A strong expression of this might be found in the Thomist 'five ways' to prove the existence of God. However, there are no indubitable proofs, and commitment to beliefs must require some kind of step beyond the evidence. Hick uses Newman's metaphor: 'the lamp of private judgement may be required to enable us to find our way; but once we have reached home we no longer need it'.[3] Faith does not rest with the evidence but with the self-authenticating nature of the church. Reasons are inevitably tentative and subject to revision, and may be proven wrong at a future date. But this is no problem for the Thomist-Catholic view, as those reasons are only like a ladder or lamp that brings us to faith. Those of us who have arrived, even if by a faulty ladder, find a certain resting place, and the ladder can be thrown away.

This account of faith is summarised by Hick in terms of three components. Firstly, the account is *intellectualist*, as it identifies faith with belief in intellectual propositions. Secondly, the account is *fideistic*, because faith is grounded in a self-authenticating source. Thirdly, the account is *voluntaristic*, as faith is an uncompelled act of the will that goes further than the force of the evidence.

This model of faith entails a particular concept of revelation. Faith and revelation are correlative terms: for the human response (faith) is to the divine disclosure (revelation). Hick describes the Thomist-Catholic view of revelation as the divine communication of verbally expressed truths to human beings. The content of this

---

[2] Hick, *Faith and Knowledge*, 13.
[3] Hick, *Faith*, 22.

communication, then, preserved in the Bible, is necessary for salvation; so faith amounts to trust in the truths of verbal revelation.

Hick does not expressly state, at least in his early work, his exact
objections to the Thomist-Catholic view he outlines. Rather than
providing clear critical objections he notes that the 'notion of
divinely revealed propositions has virtually disappeared from
Protestant theology'.[4] There is an assumption that because the view
has less support it is therefore less tenable. Certainly, in the late
1950s there was little defence of propositional revelation among
theologians, particularly in England. However, as we shall discuss in
Chapter 9, there is great strength in this position, to which Hick
does not adequately respond. One can note here that a major cause
of Hick's rejection of the propositional account of faith is simply
that he holds a different view of revelation.

Faith as Interpretation

We have already seen that faith is a correlate term to revelation.
Hick's concept of revelation is not one of divinely spoken truths but
of divine presence. Revelation is the felt presence of divine reality.
Consequently, faith, as a correlate to revelation, is 'man's awareness
of God'.[5] Faith is similar to any other form of perceptual experience.
We become conscious of things, people and God either by experiencing their presence or by inferring their presence from other
evidence. According to this account faith is not a unique category of
knowledge distinct from any other form of experience. Hick's
understanding of faith is as the pattern or structure of all knowledge.
If we are to know anything at all, then we must experience reality in
a particular way and this will require a personal response.

There are two factors relevant to this response. The first is that
the natural world has 'significance' for us. The second is that we
engage in 'interpretation' as we make sense of the world and relate
to it in an appropriate way.[6] The world always presents itself to us as
significant in some way. If it did not we would only experience

---

[4] Hick, *Faith*, 30.
[5] Hick, *Faith*, 95.
[6] Hick, *Faith*, 96–7.

chaos and confusion. Significance is not some optional extra that we might impose on the world from time to time: there is no other way to experience reality than to see it as having significance for us. In order to see such significance it is necessary for our own mind to play a part. In a subconscious way, our mind orders and structures reality so that we can make sense of it and see its significance. It is interesting to note that even at this very early stage of Hick's thought he expressed his sympathy with a Kantian form of episte-mology (we shall consider Kant's influence in later chapters). At this stage, Hick simply notes, 'In its most general form at least, we must accept the Kantian thesis that we can be aware only of that which enters into a certain framework of basic relations which is correlated with the structure of our own consciousness.'[7]

When we describe the significance of reality we are also describ-ing the way the mind orders experience. A basic 'assumption' of the subconscious is that the world is intelligible and so we respond to it accordingly. The role of the mind is inseparable from the intelligi-bility of the universe. It is significant because we see it so. The role of the mind is graphically illustrated when there is a failure or break-down. Oliver Sacks, in one of his accounts of psychological disorders, describes a man who mistook his wife for a hat.[8] In this example, the relationship between a man and his hat/wife became distorted. However, it is not that the world had lost all meaning for the man and turned to chaos; rather, the significance of the world had changed and the man was now operating with a different con-ception of reality than that of his wife, doctor, and most other humans. However outlandish an ordering of the universe may become, the mind will still order information and make some sense of reality. Ordering experience and identifying significance is a basic, unavoidable function of the mind. Furthermore, there is no view of reality from nowhere: either our mind orders the universe or we have no experience of the universe at all.

Hick describes 'interpretation' as the subjective correlative of 'significance'. This reveals an interesting way of distinguishing between subjectivity and objectivity. In common language use, we often describe the 'subjective' as the work of the mind and the

---

[7] Hick, *Faith*, 98.
[8] Sacks, *The Man who Mistook his Wife for a Hat*, 7–21.

'objective' as the independent facts of the world. This is not how these words work in Hick's scheme: both subjectivity and objectivity rely on the work of the mind. Objectivity is no more than the world *as we know it*; the mind is at work in every step of knowledge. In a formal sense, both significance and interpretation are subjective components of our knowledge, though the former seems to have its source outside our own imaginings. The implication of this point is that while Hick describes his epistemology in terms of the subject/object distinction, nonetheless both subjectivity and objectivity exist only in relation to the knowing subject. There is no distinct, objective reality accessible to the human mind. What we have access to has already been shaped by our minds.

There are two forms of interpretation distinguished by Hick. Firstly, there is interpretation as *explanation*, where an attempt is made to address why something is or is not the case. This is similar to our ordinary language use of the word, which suggests a kind of second-order activity. In this sense, we might speak of an interpretation of a Shakespearean play as an explanation. Scientific theories would also be explanations of reality, and thus secondary forms of interpretation. However, the second form of interpretation Hick distinguishes means something like *recognition*. This implies an immediate epistemic act of recognising something when it is presented to our senses. Recognition includes the interpretation of things as animals, buses, houses or people. This is no less an act of interpretation than the interpretation of a Shakespearean play. The difference in this second form of interpretation is that it is not second order, but is a primary, instinctive response to our environment. It is immediate, but still involves the work of the mind. It is interpretation as recognition that Hick uses as a key to understanding all knowledge.

Interpretation and Awareness

An important theme, which we touched on in Chapter 1, is that of levels of interpretation. Some things, such as buildings, may require only a simple level of interpretation, whereas other things, such as moral feelings, demand more complex interpretation. This pattern of interpretation may be imagined as a simple staircase. There are three steps on this staircase and each builds and relies upon the earlier steps.

The first step is the simple level of interpretation where we might recognise a book as a red rectangle. The second step interprets the red rectangle as a bound document. The third, complex, step interprets the document as a narrative story. Each step of the staircase represents a higher or more complex level of interpretation than those that went before. Each step presupposes the previous, less complex, level of interpretation. The higher steps also superimpose a new dimension of reality on the lower levels of interpretation.

Moving beyond simple interpretation, all objects appear with situational significance. This is clearly shown in the example of the book. No one could interpret the meaning of a book without knowledge of the cultural and linguistic situation in which the book is found. Therefore, every act of interpretation presupposes a web of other related interpretations. This is the situational significance of all items of knowledge. This three-step pattern of knowledge is applicable to all acts of knowing, whether a simple act of finding a vacuum cleaner, or a complex act of interpreting Old English literature.

Our interpretation of reality is also shaped by what Hick calls our *focal awareness*: we are not aware of everything going on in our immediate situation; only certain things have significance for us and hold our focal awareness. This becomes apparent when something else catches our attention and we are distracted from the object of our focal awareness. Perhaps we are reading a book and not aware of music playing in the room until a familiar song catches our attention. Then our focal awareness shifts from the meaning of the book to the sounds of the music. This theme of focal awareness is important because it indicates how little of our environment we are really attentive to. Our limited minds must be selective and focus on those things that concern us – to take in everything would overload our minds. The concept of focal awareness reminds us that our minds are active even when we are not directly aware of it.

Hick describes situational awareness as threefold: *nature, man* and *God*. These three areas of awareness correlate with the three-step staircase. Our first, simple, step of interpretation involves our awareness of the natural world in which we live and need to survive. The second step of interpretation concerns human and social relationships in which we find moral significance. The third step encompasses both previous levels, but moves beyond to include openness to a divine reality of ultimate concern. The order and relationship of the three steps in this epistemology are not accidental. Each level of awareness presupposes and interpenetrates the previous ones. Consequently, levels cannot really be isolated from each other. There is no other way, in this epistemology, but to climb the stair of knowledge from the natural realm, through the human realm and, through both of these realms, to the divine. This sequence is significant because it gives a certain priority to natural knowledge over religious knowledge. When we later turn to religious pluralism we shall see the significance of the priority given to natural knowledge. It provides a basis for Hick's claim that there is a common, prior vantage point from which the adherents of various religions may view their traditions and beliefs.

Interpretation is necessary at every level of knowledge. Sometimes we might think that reality just appears the way it is and that interpretation is only necessary when dealing with complex matters. Hick points out how naïve such an idea is. Even the simplest experience involves an interpretation of reality in order to render it meaningful to us. It is true that at the level of natural knowledge such interpretation is normally 'an unconscious and habitual process'.[9] How we interpret reality is revealed by our behaviour. Behaviour demonstrates the way in which we think we should relate to situations. We may see how this is so at each step of interpretation.

The first step of interpretation involves appropriately relating ourselves to the *natural significance of the world*. At this stage there is actually little scope for varied interpretations. People may claim to interpret physical objects or situations as they wish, but the appropriateness of those interpretations will easily be put to the test by our environment. Returning to our example from the case study of Oliver Sacks, the man who interprets his wife as his hat fails to live appropriately in relation both to his spouse and to his hat. The structure of the world does not permit much variation in interpretation. If one interprets the rain outside as sunshine and leaves the building without protection then one gets wet. There is little scope for pluralism in matters of natural knowledge.

---

[9] Hick, *Faith*, 108.

The second step of interpretation is that of *finding moral signifi-cance in the world*: 'It is characteristic of mankind to live not only in terms of the natural significance of his world but also in the dimen-sion of personality and responsibility.'[10] Our response to the moral dimension of situations includes our sense of obligation to act in a particular way. This second step provides a new context for our first step of interpretation. The world is not simply bricks, rain and bod-ies, but is a moral reality in which people should be treated in particular ways. To see a person lying in the road bleeding from an injury may only be an interpretation at the level of natural signifi-cance. However, to respond to this person as someone in need of our help is to take the second step of interpretation. We see the moral significance of our situation. Hick rests his case on situations of interpersonal relationships. Presumably, on Hick's thesis, if one were to feel ethical obligations towards animals, then this is either because the well-being of people is ultimately at stake, or because one has personified animals in some way. Ethical obligation towards the inanimate environment would also be explained by either of these motives.

Hick describes the relationship between natural and moral levels of significance as an interpenetration of one another. The latter is certainly more complex than the former but is only made possible on the basis of the first step: 'ethical significance is mediated to us in and through the natural world'.[11] An important difference between these two levels is the extent to which the interpretation we make is voluntary. The natural level of interpretation gives little room for variation; however, the ethical level allows much more scope for diverse interpretations. Situations that demand moral responses provoke a variety of ways in which humans act and, in some cir-cumstances, it may be hard to judge who has chosen the more moral behaviour.

The third step or level of interpretation brings us to the *founda-tions for religious belief*. This is the level of religious significance and, just as the ethical interpenetrates the natural level, so now the reli-gious level interpenetrates both previous steps. This is why the picture of the staircase is useful in describing Hick's position. Each

---

[10] Hick, *Faith*, 111.
[11] Hick, *Faith*, 112.

step in the staircase rests on all those preceding it, and cannot exist without those preceding steps. So the religious significance of reality is mediated through natural and moral significance. Because each step interpenetrates those previous to it, Hick must declare the third step a 'total interpretation' of reality. It is the highest step we may take and implies that we recognise a divine significance in all of reality. At this stage of his thought, as expressed in *Faith and Knowledge*, Hick was working with an explicitly Christian position that we know will be heavily qualified as his work progresses. But at this early stage of his thought he describes religious significance in theistic terms. This is his description of the religious believer's step to the third level of knowledge: 'His interpretative leap carries him into a world which exists through the will of a holy, righteous, and loving Being who is the creator and sustainer of all that is.'[12]

The use of the word 'leap' at this point is instructive. Each step of interpretation is an increasingly voluntary act. As the moral interpretation implies greater cognitive freedom than the natural interpretation, so the religious interpretation will imply greater freedom still. It is not evidence that coerces us to make the religious response, but the leap of knowledge. Climbing the epistemological staircase requires initial acts of increasingly uncompelled interpretation to begin each new stage: the act of ethical interpretation was more voluntary than the natural; and the act of religious interpretation is supposed to be entirely uncompelled.

Religious faith, which is the act of interpretation at this final level, is an uncompelled act of human response to an awareness of the existence of a loving Being. This awareness is mediated through nature and conscience. Later in his work the content of that knowledge, 'a holy, righteous, and loving Being', would be substantially modified in line with the pluralist hypothesis. However, this basic pattern of epistemology would remain in force. Because we have certain moral feelings and the world around us appears in a certain way we may be led to believe that there is a loving Creator. At this stage, Hick draws upon certain theological themes to substantiate his case that religious knowledge is uncompelled. These would also need to be modified, but, in various forms, they remain part of Hick's later argument. The essential theme is that of the personal

---

[12] Hick, *Faith*, 115.

character of humanity and God. Because both God and people are in relationship, Hick supposes that the grounds of that personal relationship must be uncompelled; otherwise, it would not be a truly personal relationship at all. 'If man is to be personal, God must be *deus absconditus*. He must, so to speak, stand back, hiding himself behind his creation, and, leaving us the freedom to recognise or fail to recognise his dealings with us.'[13]

Hick claims that the only alternative to this *deus absconditus* would be a manipulative God who would coerce men and women into faith. Although the natural world is coercive (little variation in our interpretation is possible), God, unlike the natural order, 'desires, not a compelled obedience, but our uncoerced growth towards the humanity revealed in Christ'.[14] The ambiguity of the religious dimension is a necessary condition for a truly personal relationship between people and God. The role of freedom is very important at this stage of Hick's thought, and he accepts that a great variety of responses to the religious significance of the universe are possible.

Hick draws upon the work of Wittgenstein for his term 'experiencing as',[15] which describes the way in which the same reality may be experienced differently. Various factors influence the way an event or person is experienced. Some people experience reality as mediating the existence of God, others as devoid of such divine significance. Because faith is uncompelled, there is no neutral piece of evidence that could decide between these responses.[16]

That the nature of faith is to be an uncompelled response to an ambiguous religious reality raises an important problem. One might have good reason to trust in the veridical or truthful nature of claims about the natural order, as these reasons are the largely unambiguous nature of the world and the fact that such interpretations tend to be

---

[13] Hick, *Faith*, 135.

[14] Hick, *Faith*, 135.

[15] Hick, *Faith*, 142; cf. Wittgenstein, *Philosophical Investigations*, 193–213.

[16] At this early stage in his work the Bible and the historical person of Jesus remain crucial for the Christian's faith (Hick, 'Religious Faith as Experiencing-as', 46–7). However, personal experience contributes the vital factor of significance and so, for that reason, neither the Bible nor miracles could settle the dispute between believer and unbeliever.

shared by large numbers of people. Obvious empirical tests can satisfy many simple disagreements and much of the world's population has come to substantial agreement on the way our physical environment works. But religious awareness is a voluntary response to something quite ambiguous. There are no simple tests, little global agreement, and many possible variations in interpretation. This conclusion provided the seedbed for the pluralist hypothesis, but that hypothesis was yet to take root. At this stage Hick was more concerned with the negative conclusions that might be drawn from his epistemology. The apparent ambiguity of God's existence and the wide variations in human responses cast doubt on the veridical nature of religious faith. Hick, in his early work, was sensitive to this objection, particularly as posed by many atheists: perhaps there is no divine reality 'out there', but religious language simply expresses how believers feel.

Is There a God?

We have already seen Hick's commitment to a realist account of religious language. His proposed 'eschatological verification' was an attempt to establish that believers, whether right or wrong, certainly intend to say something about a reality 'out there'. But can one show that the claims of religious faith are likely or even plausible? At this stage Hick is not concerned with the question of pluralism as such, but only with the difference between theistic and atheistic belief. At the third step of interpretation there is a basic clash between naturalists and supernaturalists, and one possible route to settling such disputes would be an argument in favour of the existence of God. There are many arguments that have been proposed in the course of the centuries, but Hick is doubtful of their validity.

One of the most common theistic arguments, though itself reliant on some form of argument from design, has been stated in terms of probability. In essence, such an argument proposes that the appearance of the universe suggests it is more likely the product of an intelligent designer than not. An example of such a proposal is found in the work of Richard Swinburne who describes rational belief as that which is 'rendered probable by [the] evidence'.[17] For a

---

[17] Swinburne, *Faith and Reason*, 63.

belief to be rational, according to Swinburne, it must have a probability closer to 1 than to 0 and/or a greater probability than its alternatives. Hick's account rules out the applicability of probability arguments to religious knowledge. In particular, religious knowledge is a total interpretation of reality. This means that there is nothing else with which our knowledge may be compared – we do not have several different universes which we might compare in order to establish whether this one is likely to be the product of an intelligent designer. Probability would be inappropriate when applied to the character of the universe because the very term 'universe' implies the totality of all things. There is nothing by which such totality may be compared or measured in order to subject it to a probability test. For this reason, probability is not able to decide in favour of Christianity.

However, nor can anti-theistic arguments use probability against the Christian faith. For example, it might be suggested that the scale of evil in the world weighs against the claim that it is the product of an intelligent designer. This argument is equally faulty because we are not able to compare the evils of this universe with the evils of alternative universes. Both theism and naturalism are total interpretations of reality. The difficulty in deciding between them is not a lack of relevant information but a lack of any logical vantage point from which such an assessment could be made: 'There is no objective measuring rod by which to compare the depths to which wickedness can sink with the height to which goodness can rise, and so to balance the problem of evil, which challenges theism, against the problem of good, which challenges naturalism.'[18]

Neither the theistic nor the atheistic worldview can settle the differences between them by appeal to objective arguments or evidence. Debate between such worldviews cannot proceed purely in terms of rational argument, but ultimately requires the 'attempt to bring the other to see the universe as he himself sees it'.[19] For example, appeals by theists to the evidential value of fulfilled prophecy or answered prayer cannot settle this dispute. The 'evidence' here is really only a voluntary interpretation of ambiguous reality. The believer and the naturalist have not arrived at their perspectives

---

[18] Hick, *Faith*, 156.
[19] Hick, *Faith*, 156.

through the force of such evidence or abstract speculation, but through an experiential awareness. Much as we 'feel' a moral urgency about a situation where there is cruelty, so we could 'feel' there is a further religious dimension to such a situation. In Hick's epistemology it is experiential awareness that divides believer from unbeliever. To be conscious of reality as infused with the divine presence provides basic justification for believers to have faith in God. Similarly, though conversely, atheists may also be justified in their unbelief because they are not conscious of any such divine presence.

From Christian Faith to Religious Faith

Despite dramatic developments in Hick's theology, we have established that there is reason to consider a basic, underlying continuity to run through his work. Hick's account of faith provides an anchor for the substantial unity of his thought. But there is still a revision that Hick must make in order to maintain the compatibility of his epistemology with the pluralist hypothesis. This revision involves relocating his account of faith specific to one tradition (Christian faith) to one compatible with a plurality of traditions (we shall call this Religious faith – implying a faith not specifically related to Christianity). He is able to achieve this relocation with minimal effect on his foundational work because his view of faith was always compatible with pluralism. Nonetheless, we may now draw out what actualises a shift in Hick's position from Christian faith to Religious faith. First we shall establish just how far the early statement of his epistemology relied upon a Christian theology; then we shall note how he submerges that account into his very general category of Religious faith.

We have seen that faith is a human response to our environment and Hick claims this response brings us into relation with a unique object. As a total interpretation of our surroundings it relates us to an objectively existing God: 'enfolding and interpenetrating this interlocking mass of finite situations there is also, according to the insistent witness of theistic religion, the all-encompassing situation of being in the presence of God and within the sphere of an on-going divine purpose'.[20]

---

[20] Hick, *Faith*, 107.

This description of faith depends upon a theistic framework of interpretation in which it makes sense to speak of God being present and having purposes. Hick also emphasises the realist sense in which he identifies God as the object of faith. The God of faith is not simply 'the divine' in some vague sense, but is a personal being capable of purpose and presence. This personal nature of God we saw emphasised in Hick's account of the freedom of faith. He uses the analogy of human relationships to describe the difference between an I–It relationship and an I–Thou relationship. When we deal with other people merely as objects for our discussion, use and analysis, we treat them as an 'it'. However, true human relationships demand that we respect people as, at least similar to ourselves. The I–Thou relationship between people is structurally the same as our relationship to God. The divine being is not an object for discussion so much as a person for us to respond to. Hick's understanding of faith is based upon a concept of a personal God as the focus of faith. It is more than a merely theistic framework, because a theist need not have such a personal view of the divine being; and it is not deism either, a form of theism in which God is removed from his creation and has no relation to it. This suggests that Hick's early account of faith is grounded in an explicitly Christian framework.

Furthermore, this 'personalist' account of faith is rooted in an orthodox view of the incarnation. Hick affirms the assumption made in the study of the history of religions that religious development is evolutionary. In his early work the concept of a personal relationship with God is the pinnacle of religious experience. The history of religions has been marked by 'gradual liberation'[21] of individuals from group mentality to a sense of the personal divine mind calling those individuals into a voluntary, loving relationship. Hick points to the doctrine of the incarnation as the 'classic exemplification of this principle'.[22] Hence he describes Jesus Christ as the culmination of this gradual process of God revealing himself. 'In Christianity the catalyst of faith is the person of Jesus Christ. It is in the historical figure of Jesus Christ that, according to the

---

[21] Hick, *Faith*, 139.
[22] Hick, *Faith*, 140.

Christian claim, God has in an unique and final way disclosed himself to men.'[23]

Hick distinguishes two senses in which faith is related to Christ: faith *in* and faith *from* Christ. Faith *in* Christ is the act of interpreting the historical Jesus as the Christ. Faith *from* Christ is the resulting act of interpreting the universe in the light of that new-found Christocentric perspective. This account may be described as Christian because it relates faith directly to the person and message of the historical Jesus.

Hick also applies his account of faith to the doctrine of salvation and the relationship between faith and works. He does this in very much a Christian theological framework. While Christ's teachings concerning morality involve certain rules, nonetheless the purpose of that morality is much more than simply rule-keeping. He points out that Jesus levelled a critique against the religious establishment of the day, teaching that the 'kingdom is extended not merely by securing conformity of men's overt deeds' to the law 'but by changing people themselves'.[24] Hick argues that there is an integral connection between faith and works. Christian faith implies a new interpretation of reality which, if genuine, precipitates a radical transformation of one's very nature. Faith is not mere assent to belief, and Hick's account gives emphasis to these practical implications of Christian faith.

We have now established three distinctively Christian factors in Hick's early description of faith. Firstly, faith relates people to a personal God in an I–Thou relationship of love, presence and purpose. Secondly, faith is both exemplified by and made possible through Jesus Christ. Thirdly, faith is revealed in a life transformed by the teachings of Christ. However, none of these factors is essential to his account of faith. Underlying this apparently Christian account is a more neutral description of faith. I shall now summarise this general account of religious faith that underlies even Hick's most early work. This will then provide a bridge for us to cross into the epistemology of his later work. It will become apparent that this bridge is not long, as his basic

---

[23] Hick, *Faith*, 216. This work includes a defence of the orthodox doctrine of the incarnation, 219–28.

[24] Hick, *Faith*, 241.

theory of knowledge was always compatible with pluralism and never dependent on Christian theology.

From Religious Faith to Non-Religious Faith

Hick's early work discussed the existence of God in terms of atheism, agnosticism and theism: he claimed his epistemology could cover both the belief of Christian and atheist. While these are distinct worldviews, they nonetheless share important features. At least in Hick's use, they share a monotheistic framework where either the one God exists or does not exist. Hick discusses epistemology only in relation to the supposed awareness of one God, rather than any idea of there being many gods. The framework of his account is monotheistic rather than polytheistic. Furthermore, he admits the field of his enquiry to be limited to the Judaeo-Christian tradition: 'For this book is not a comprehensive treatment of the place of faith in the religions of the world, but only an essay on the epistemology of faith as it occurs in that form of religion which constitutes a live option for most of the participants in our Western stream of culture.'[25]

This may suggest that Hick is committed to developing an epistemology that is specific to the Christian tradition. However, this is not the case, and the 'live option' he describes is primarily an illustration of his theory. While the theories of faith with which Hick engages have arisen within the Christian tradition, the framework in which he conducts his discussion is quite neutral. The terms are psychological or philosophical and not dependent on any particular theology. The epistemological structure that Hick outlines in no way depends upon there being true Christian revelation. The purpose of his work is to outline a philosophically neutral categorisation of the religious mind. It is true that in his early work Hick assumes Christianity to be the best or highest exemplification of faith, but this has no bearing on his proposal.

One indication of the fact that Christianity illustrates rather than determines Hick's thesis is found in his use of Scripture in *Faith and Knowledge*. In a work on philosophy it is not necessarily a fault for a

---

[25] Hick, *Faith*, 2.

Christian author to make little or no reference to Scripture. However, Hick does choose to use Scripture and, therefore, the way he does so is revealing. The Bible is quoted directly eighty-three times in this book. Of these, eighty are to be found in the final part where he brings his theory to bear on Christian belief. Just three quotes appear in the bulk of the work in which he proposes the foundations for belief. This is not a criticism in itself, but it does show the kind of relationship Hick assumes between Christianity and philosophy. His philosophical account is certainly illustrated by features of the Christian faith (the final part of his book), but it does not arise from them. His account of how we come to know God is based on general, neutral categories of thought, which could be acceptable to believer and non-believer alike.

The most noticeable feature of Hick's early epistemology is its emphasis on a direct experience of religious significance in the world around rather than in historical claims. This suggests to Helm that Hick's position is not really a description of Christian faith: 'Though Hick's model of religious knowledge as cognition-in-experience *might* work for certain cases it is not appropriate as a model for religious belief as it operates in a historically-grounded religion such as Christianity.'[26] Hick's concept of the knowledge of God relies upon an experiential awareness of the divine rather than historic revelation or miracles. Even at this stage in his work it is open to question whether this epistemology is particularly useful in describing Christian faith.

We shall now move on to a consideration of a much later presentation of Hick's epistemology. In this later account his intention is to make a defence of the pluralist hypothesis, rather than of Christian theism, and, given his philosophical framework, this transition is relatively easily made. Just as the Christian faith was primarily illustrative of his general account of Religious faith, so too are the faiths of many religions. Indeed, a pluralist view of the relationship between the religions seems to fit more comfortably with this epistemology than orthodox Christian theology ever did.

---

[26] Helm, *Varieties*, 156.

Chapter 4

Ambiguity and Scepticism

The Ambiguity of the Universe

In *An Interpretation of Religion* Hick, drawing upon his long-established epistemology, presents a detailed argument for his pluralist hypothesis. What we now find is not a great amendment being made to his early work, but, rather, a simplification of it to its logical essence. The Christian superstructure is stripped away to reveal its foundations.

Hick continues to maintain that the universe is religiously ambiguous, meaning that we are not morally or logically compelled to adopt any particular interpretation of it. This ambiguity is not peculiar to religious belief but is part of the very structure of human knowledge. We are never able to get beyond or outside the way things appear to us, and so there cannot be absolute certainty that the meaning we impose on the universe (by an act of interpretation) is correct. Nonetheless, the meaning we see will determine our lifestyle in relation to our world. Just as religious belief, if genuine, inspires a certain kind of lifestyle, so our beliefs about the natural world will inspire certain kinds of behaviour. It is possible to examine how appropriate our beliefs are by the pragmatic test of whether they enable us to live effectively in the world, or whether they destroy us. For example, beliefs about which mushrooms are edible and which are not illustrates this point. We might be free to choose to believe all kinds of things about mushrooms and never be sure that our beliefs are entirely correct. However, eating certain mushrooms will still kill us, while others will be entirely benign. In this way, there is only a very narrow band of parameters regarding what might constitute viable natural meaning in the universe: 'Thus at this level our cognitive freedom is minimal; the physical world compels us to interpret its signals correctly and to live in it in terms of its real meaning for beings such as ourselves.'[1]

In this manner, Hick establishes an important connection between interpretation and experience. Our interpretations of the universe are not the result of guesswork or imagination alone. If they were, we could make disastrous decisions. No, our interpretations result from our engagement with and experience of the world. Experience is the key factor in knowledge, and its prominence develops during the course of Hick's work.

As we have seen, Hick introduced the term 'experiencing-as' into the second edition of *Faith and Knowledge*. It is offered as a term of clarification for his work rather than as a revision of it. Hick adopts the term from Wittgenstein's notion of 'seeing-as', though he applies the concept more broadly to cover not just odd moments of experience but all experience. There is ambiguity in even the simplest natural situation, but we do not notice it because the subconscious processes of the mind actively deal with that ambiguity.

As already mentioned, at the level of religious knowledge the universe exhibits greater ambiguity than at the level of natural knowledge. While for Christians it is Christ who is the object of faith, other traditions have alternative foci. The world process is itself the object of Buddhist faith, open to reinterpretation as either the 'stream of life, death and rebirth' or 'in a radically different way it is Nirvana!'[2] So we see the same process at work. An otherwise ambiguous reality finds order and meaning through the interpretative faculties of faith. It is a basic religious experience that causes men and women to interpret the universe in religious terms.

In Hick's earlier work we saw that Christianity provided primary illustrative material for his thesis. In his later work he distances his thesis from any particular tradition and offers an account that can be illustrated by any of the major world religions. All traditions are acting as the filters of reality, overwhelming data would otherwise make coherent knowledge impossible. This is Hick's explanation of the common function of religions. However different their concepts and images, they all function as filters of ultimate or divine

---

[1] Hick, *An Interpretation of Religion*, 137.
[2] Hick, *Interpretation*, 157.

reality so that our finite minds can make some sense of the religious dimension. Christianity provides neither a unique nor a supreme source of knowledge.

Hick's three-step epistemology is retained in his later work and proves entirely compatible with this more general account of faith. Indeed, the idea that the third step involves complete cognitive freedom because in no sense does the religious dimension coerce our response, leads inevitably to the pluralist case. Given limited freedom at the second step we are led to expect that there will be various moral theories and aspirations in the world, though also an underlying continuity on major moral themes. This is exactly what we find. There are very different moralities in the world and yet also remarkable consistency over issues like murder or adultery. Therefore, one is led to expect that the much greater cognitive freedom at the level of religious knowledge will be mirrored by much greater variation in religious beliefs. It follows that the diversity of the world religions can be used as evidence for the validity of Hick's epistemology!

We have already noted the theological reasons Hick gave for this cognitive freedom. Truly personal relationships must not be compelled if they are to remain personal. Because God desires that men and women exercise their free will in choosing to love him, Hick describes God, in his earlier work, as 'hiding himself behind his creation'.[3] If God were to provide incontrovertible proof of his existence then this would amount to manipulation and coercion. However, this theological line of argument is too dependent on the Christian tradition, and consequently no longer carries the same weight in Hick's work. In order to sustain the case for a pluralist interpretation of religion, Hick has to provide a fresh treatment of the ambiguity of the universe and this he does in *An Interpretation of Religion*. This fresh treatment tries to make sense of ambiguity without relying on a Christian doctrine of God and freedom.

Hick continues to maintain that the basic ambiguity of the universe explains why it may be interpreted in either religious or naturalistic ways. It is only the Enlightenment that has made this perspective possible. Prior to the Enlightenment period the west

---

[3] Hick, *Interpretation*, 135.

was dominated by the Catholic and Protestant versions of Christendom, which gave a certain coherence to people's worldviews. Only in the wake of the Enlightenment have various forms of naturalism become plausible: 'in this post-Enlightenment age of doubt we have realised that the universe is religiously ambiguous. It evokes and sustains non-religious as well as religious responses'.[4] God, if there is a God, continues to make himself scarce.

Hick outlines a very radical position on the ambiguity of the universe. He is not simply making the weak point that the universe, as a matter of empirical fact, is interpreted in various ways and that, therefore, its meaning is ambiguous. Everyone agrees that there are many, contradictory interpretations of the universe, but that sense of plurality or ambiguity is of little consequence. Hick is making the point that the universe is necessarily like that. This in turn means that many interpretations will be equally rational and defensible. There will never be conclusive arguments in favour of one interpretation over all others – ambiguity is written into the very fabric of things.

For this reason arguments for and against the existence of God or a transcendental reality can never be conclusive. Hick maintains his belief that theistic arguments are unsatisfactory as far as public debate is concerned. Some have a limited role in the believer's own life in confirming a religious experience, but none is likely to settle any arguments in the life of someone lacking that experience. Religious experience itself is only compelling for those who have it. Hick points out that it is perfectly rational for the naturalist to claim that 'the feeling of an unseen presence could all be hallucinatory in character'.[5]

Of course, the reverse continues to be true too: naturalistic arguments against theism are also inconclusive. The approaches of Freud and Durkheim to religion challenge theism with their claim that religion can be satisfactorily explained without any reference to supernatural activity. However, each is a case of reductionism that depends 'upon a prior naturalistic conviction'.[6] In a mirror image of the believer's predicament, the naturalist already has a sense or

---

[4] Hick, *Interpretation*, 74.

[5] Hick, *Interpretation*, 102.

[6] Hick, *Interpretation*, 114.

conviction about the way things are that determines his or her interpretation of the evidence. What Hick concludes is that everyone
should accept the basic ambiguity of the universe. Yes, everyone
will have convictions and experiences that they personally find
compelling, but no one should claim absolute truth for his or her
own interpretation. 'It seems, then, that the universe maintains its
inscrutable ambiguity. In some aspects it invites, whilst in others it
repels a religious response. It permits both a religious and a naturalistic faith, but haunted in each case by a contrary possibility that can
never be exorcised.'[7]

This ambiguity of the universe provides the basis for a relaunch
of Hick's somewhat simplified theory of religious knowledge. Faith
is the act of interpretation by which human beings order the ambiguous data of the universe into a sense and meaning that reveal a
supernatural reality behind it all. Those without faith are still
engaged in the act of interpretation, though their worldview leads
them to a perspective on life that lacks divine significance.

The fundamental ambiguity of the universe provides the
epistemic basis for Hick's religious pluralism. Indeed, his account
would lead one to expect a multiplicity of interpretations. Not only
are there positions of naturalism and supernaturalism, but supernaturalism is itself divided into myriad forms of response to divine
reality. According to Hick, the data of the universe lends itself to
any of these interpretations.

The Place of Conviction

The relationship between faith and the apparent ambiguity of the
universe gives rise to an important tension. Hick is distinguishing
between our logical grasp of what the universe is like and our felt
experience of the universe. According to our logical or formal
grasp, at least since the Enlightenment, the universe is religiously
ambiguous. However, the concrete character of our experience of
the universe is largely unambiguous. This is why religious convictions can be so strong. The universe just seems that way. Most
religious people will interpret the universe in a particular way and

---

[7] Hick, *Interpretation*, 124.

will not feel that it is ambiguous. Their intuition or sense of what the universe is like seems to confirm their religious beliefs.

Furthermore, many atheists also feel that the universe has a particular concrete character. Only in the formal, logical sense does Hick urge us to accept the religious ambiguity of the universe. He does not mean that religious people should give up their confidence and actually feel the ambiguity of the universe. This is primarily because it is only possible to adopt one particular world-view as a live option at any given time: 'For whilst the objective ambiguity of our environment consists in the fact that it is capable of being interpreted in a variety of ways, its consciously experienced and actively lived-in character consists in its actually being interpreted as meaningful in a particular way which, whilst it operates, excludes other possible ways.'[8]

The tension in this relationship between faith and ambiguity is that, in order to adopt the pluralist hypothesis, one must be simultaneously aware of the religious ambiguity of the universe as a matter of fact, while remaining emotionally convinced that the universe is religiously unambiguous. The argument is that for philosophical reasons one should accept ambiguity, even though for psychological (or intuitive) reasons one cannot accept such ambiguity. This distinction possibly explains how Hick continues to maintain that he is both a practising Christian, indeed a Christian minister, and is also a proponent of religious pluralism. He is able to share in the Christian and devotional life, for all practical purposes, but is also able to suspend that commitment in favour of his pluralist proposal when considering the phenomenon of religion in strictly philosophical terms. In order to do this he simply needs to isolate theology and philosophy as distinct modes of thought, and can then claim to be a Christian theologian and a pluralist philosopher.

However, we have already noted that philosophy does not operate in this way in Hick's thought. While for much of Christian history, philosophy has been a subservient discipline, under the judgement of theology, in Hick's thought philosophy is the primary discipline – philosophy must determine and drive theology. This is exactly how the tension between ambiguity and conviction is resolved in his work. The pluralist hypothesis, being philosophy, is

---

[8] Hick, *Interpretation*, 129.

offered as an all-inclusive interpretation of particular religious patterns of belief and behaviour. It cannot be excluded from extending its revolutionary impulse to the devotional life of believers. Philosophical conclusions have a primary status and they stand in judgement over theological ideas.

For this reason, every religious believer must appropriate the implications of the ambiguity of the universe to his or her own faith. As Hick wrote earlier, 'It is for the adherents of each of the great traditions to look critically at their own dogmas in the light of their new experience within a religiously plural world.'[9] Thus for Christians it is their commitment to the uniqueness or superiority of Christ that must be reformed in the light of pluralism.[10] Philosophy determines theology. Hick's resolution of the tension between the convictions of faith and the ambiguity of the universe is really to place the role of commitment in a new context. Religious commitments must be suspended in favour of a more basic admission that religious pluralism is true. This suspension of commitment has led to Hick's pluralism being described as 'transcendental agnosticism'.[11]

Is Hick an agnostic? Of course, he would profess not to be. He believes that there is a transcendent Ultimate Reality that is the real ground of human religious experience. However, in philosophical terms, Hick is willing to suspend this belief. His epistemology is founded on the assumption that we can have no absolute certainty regarding ultimate reality. It will be helpful at this point to compare Hick's epistemology with another philosophical school: scepticism. The parallels will be instructive.

---

[9] Hick, *Problems of Religious Pluralism*, 50.

[10] A point made over the years by many critics of Hick. See e.g., Forrester, 'Professor Hick and the Universe of Faiths', 72; Netland, *Dissonant Voices*, 240–49; and Ogden, 'Problems in the Case for a Pluralistic Theology of Religions', 503–7.

[11] In D'Costa, 'John Hick and Religious Pluralism: Yet Another Revolution'; Mase, 'Does Hick's Post-Copernican Pluralism in *An Interpretation of Religion* lead to Agnosticism?'; and also developed in D'Costa, *The Meeting of Religions and the Trinity*. Peter Byrne identified earlier expressions of Hick's pluralist case as both sceptic and agnostic; 'John Hick's Philosophy of World Religions', 292.

The Sceptic Tradition

Terence Penelhum surveys the tradition of scepticism from its origins in ancient Greek philosophy, taking 'Pyrrhonian' scepticism
as the classic example. This school sought to demonstrate that
there simply is no clinching argument in favour of any dogmatic
convictions. In particular, the certainty with which the rival Greek
schools of Epicureans and Stoics held to their doctrines was not
justified. According to the sceptics, such certitude is not possible
because of the 'incapacity of human reason'.[12] The chief purpose of
the sceptic movement was to help people to recognise the limitations of reason. However, the sceptics did not simply leave their
followers in a state of intellectual doubt, but sought to provide a
practical way of living with doubt. To the Greeks, scepticism was
offered as a practical philosophy. Penelhum describes the sceptic as
a philosopher who, while doubting everything, nonetheless lived
in conformity to cultural norms, though 'in an undogmatic, or un-
committed, or belief-less way'.[13] There are habits of life that help
one to live as if a range of presuppositions were true, even though,
at a theoretical level and in philosophical discussion, one must admit that such certainty has no foundation.

Hick does not acknowledge any connection between his ambiguity thesis and the methodology of the sceptics. However, a
description of the sceptic methodology will make clear how similar
his thought is to that of the sceptics.

> the Sceptic will assemble all those arguments that Dogmatists have
> used to show that it not only appears that *p*, but really is, and then will
> assemble all the arguments that contrary-minded Dogmatists have
> used to show that even if it appears that *p*, it is not; this assemblage will
> bring upon him an incapacity to judge either that *p*, or that not-*p*. This
> will not make it cease to appear to him that *p* . . . but it will enable him
> to live with his fellows who insist that *p* by conforming in his actions to
> their beliefs without affirming them.[14]

---

[12] Penelhum, *God and Skepticism*, 4.
[13] Penelhum, *Skepticism*, 6.
[14] Penelhum, *Skepticism*, 9.

Hick and the sceptics both develop a system of methodological doubt whereby no particular proposition may be held to be entirely certain. This is because of the important distinction between reality as it really is and reality as it appears to us. How then should we live? Hick shares with the sceptics a common approach to life. One must suspend judgement on the validity of any given worldview and yet act from day to day as if one particular worldview were true. For practical reasons, the chosen worldview would usually turn out to be the worldview that dominates one's culture or parents. The practice of setting arguments for *p* and for not-*p* off against one another is a simple method for undermining confidence in any absolute truth. Exactly such a method is found in Hick's approach to arguments for and against theism and naturalism.[15]

The realisation that the true nature of the universe is ambiguous does not leave one's worldview unchanged. While the sceptics might share the same cultural norms and general worldview as their Greek neighbours, they held those beliefs in a very different way. The sceptics now return to the beliefs of their culture but 'disinfected' of 'those specious underpinnings of belief and valuation that have given it meaning'.[16] The sceptics had come to realise that unravelling the ambiguity of the universe was neither possible nor necessary for a content life. Penelhum uses the term 'quietude' to describe the kind of conformity to tradition engaged in by the sceptic. His or her way of life 'was one in which quietude could come from recognising that the world which he and others like him inhabited was one in which we could live satisfactorily by assenting to appearances but not disputing about the realities which lay behind them'.[17]

Hick makes a similar claim regarding the way we should hold our religious commitments given the religious ambiguity of the universe. In the wake of his Copernican revolution Hick continued to claim to be a Christian and follow Christian practices, but only because they help one to live in an appropriate way, not because Christianity can reveal anything beyond the world of appearances. For a pluralist, creedal confessions may still be professed but they are

---

[15] The structure of Hick's argument in *Interpretation*, 73–125.

[16] Penelhum, *Skepticism*, 10.

[17] Penelhum, *Skepticism*, 11.

held only as secondary, poetic expressions, not as absolute truths. Therefore Hick's continued profession of Christian commitment must be understood in the light of an epistemology in which truth is relativised.

The assumption that the universe is religiously ambiguous changes our attitudes to the beliefs we have. Hick's ambiguity thesis throws all inter-religious dialogue and apologetics into a new context. Debate and disputes must be approached neither with strong convictions nor as if one has true answers, but rather as one in humble ignorance who is continually searching for a truth that will always lie just out of reach. Dialogue, on this model, is always truth-seeking and never truth-announcing. Such an approach is common to most pluralists. For example, Ian Markham bases his argument for 'open' religious dialogue on the claim that 'We now accept that absolute certainty about the nature of the world is clearly unobtainable.'[18] Keith Ward's argument for 'convergent pluralism' also shares this basic approach.[19] The sceptic approach to life follows quite naturally from this epistemology. Religious belief must be understood as a matter of opinion informing day-to-day devotion and lifestyle, even though one's deeper conviction is that the universe is religiously silent and open to a range of equally plausible interpretations. Hick is an agnostic in this sceptic sense.

The Place of Coercion

Hick's argument for the religious ambiguity of the universe stems partly from his idea that for a belief to be freely held it must occur without coercion. In his three-step model of knowledge we noted that each step implies a greater degree of cognitive freedom. There were particular theological concerns that also motivated this commitment to the importance of freedom. Because the divine was, at least for the early Hick, a personal being, so it was important that

---

[18] Markham, *Plurality and Christian Ethics*, 176.

[19] Ward, *A Vision to Pursue*, 175–7. Of course, such statements as those of Markham and Ward point to the inner contradiction of the sceptical method; its certainty about uncertainty. This is a contradiction to which we shall return in relation to the work of Hick.

our human response was freely given: a genuine relationship between personal beings must not be coerced. In later writing, Penelhum has pointed out that Hick's approach to coercion is mistaken. Hick confuses 'having the truth made clear to one with being shattered into submission'.[20] Having the truth made clear to one (for example, through reason, revelation or miracles) removes any grounds for reasonable doubt, but does not restrict human freedom. Any human subject is free to reject those evidences. It is true that such behaviour is irrational, but Penelhum points out that this is irrelevant. One may choose to act irrationally and, in so doing, one is exercising cognitive freedom. Paul Helm also argues against Hick's account by pointing out that one may freely believe on the basis of evidence: 'Another alternative is to believe in God, and to obey God because it is thought that there are good grounds for believing in and obeying him. And if someone has good grounds (as he thinks) this need not imply that this obedience is compelled either in the sense that it is heteronomous or that it is accompanied by feelings of compulsion or constraint.'[21]

Helm argues that one must distinguish between the factors that amount to compulsion and the grounds that might be felt by the believer to constitute overwhelming reasons to believe in God. If we believe because of the weight of evidence we are still acting freely and remain responsible for our beliefs. Indeed, Hick provides a good example of such valid 'coerced' faith in his description of Christ. Despite the dramatic revisions in his Christology, a clear pattern emerges in his description of what kind of faith Jesus had. In his early work we read, 'For in whatever manner Jesus first impressed his disciples – whether as a wonder-worker, as a teacher, or as a magnetic and numinous personality – the outstanding fact about him, which soon gripped them, was his sheer moral goodness and purity, his total lack of concern for himself and the absolute dedication of his life to his heavenly Father's purposes.'[22] In this account of Christ, Hick uses the words 'sheer', 'total' and 'absolute'

---

[20] Penelhum, 'Reflections on the Ambiguity of the World' in Sharma (ed.), *God, Truth and Reality: Essays in Honour of John Hick*, 172. This relates to his account of scepticism in Penelhum, *Skepticism*, 111–12.

[21] Helm, *The Varieties of Belief*, 152.

[22] Hick, *God Has Many Names*, 223.

to stress the quality of faith and conviction that motivated him. This was a man consumed with the sense of God's will and purpose. There is no hint that Jesus had come to make a reasonable choice in the face of an ambiguous universe. This characterisation of Jesus continues to be made in Hick's contribution to *The Myth of God Incarnate*. Here he describes Jesus as 'intensely and overwhelmingly conscious of the reality of God' and 'his life a continuous response to the divine love as both utterly gracious and utterly demanding'.[23] Hick does not describe Jesus as exercising cognitive freedom in his response to God, but as being 'overwhelmingly conscious' of the truth of theism, and finding God's love 'utterly demanding'.

In Hick's last attempt at an orthodox statement of the identity of Jesus, called the *Agapē*-Christology, he sought to define the oneness of God and Christ in terms of their common commitment to the divine will. He describes this relationship as 'analogous to that in which the radiating energy of the sun "causes" the falling of its rays upon the earth's surface'.[24] Again, the emphasis is upon the overwhelming sense of God in the life of Jesus. It does not seem that Jesus was freely responding to an ambiguous situation. The account of the faith of Jesus in *An Interpretation of Religion* sets it alongside the faith of many holy people in many religions. Regarding Jesus, Hick notes that 'it was entirely rational to believe that God is real; and indeed that it would have been irrational on his part not to'.[25] A freely given response to a religiously ambiguous universe does not seem to be characteristic of the faith of Jesus. In the more recent *The Metaphor of God Incarnate* we find one of the strongest statements of Christ's convictions: 'From the point of view of the psychology of religion we can say that only an extremely intense God-consciousness could have sustained Jesus' firm prophetic assurance and charismatic power. The heavenly Father was utterly real to him – as real as the men and women with whom he interacted every day or the Galilean hills among which they lived.'[26]

This description raises some perplexing problems for understanding Hick's epistemology. According to this description, the

---

[23] Hick, *The Myth of God Incarnate*, 172.
[24] Hick, *God*, 163.
[25] Hick, *Interpretation*, 216.
[26] Hick, *The Metaphor of God Incarnate*, 18.

reality of God was no different to Jesus than the reality of the hills. We noted that a primary distinction between the first step in Hick's epistemology, the interpretation of nature, and the third step, the interpretation of religious reality, is that higher steps permit greater variation. In *Faith and Knowledge* we were given a moral ground for this distinction: 'If God were to reveal himself to us in the coercive way in which the physical world is disclosed to us, he would thereby annihilate us as free and responsible persons.'[27] This implies that the response of Jesus and the great saints[28] to God involved the annihilation of their freedom. The vividness of the religious experience of Jesus made it analogous to our natural experience of the world and, therefore, devoid of real freedom. Elsewhere Hick describes the faith of Jesus as 'involuntary'.[29]

Hick's treatment of faith and certainty are inconsistent. He commends the faith of Jesus as the exemplary model for Christians and yet his faith is an example of compelled belief. Therefore Hick's own account disproves his notion that religious belief must be uncompelled. Jesus, were he the only figure in history to have done so, would be the exception that proves the rule. Furthermore, Jesus is not unique according to Hick, but one of a number of holy people who shared this form of faith. This great cloud of witnesses proves that there is nothing incoherent in a free moral agent adopting a religious belief, even though compelled to do so by reason, revelation or miracles. Of course, it is true that 'compulsion' in this sense does not imply being violently forced to believe. This is the point that Penelhum made in noting that Hick confuses being shattered into submission with having the truth shown to one. There really is no incompatibility between compulsion and freedom: we are responsible for our choices and beliefs, even if we feel compelled to believe them.

---

[27] Hick, *Faith and Knowledge*, 134.

[28] In 'Religious Faith as Experiencing-as' Hick prefers the term 'great souls' because the word 'saint' might suggest only the significant holy people from the Christian tradition. I shall use the term 'great saints' but I mean 'saint' in Hick's terms – an exemplary religious person from any tradition.

[29] Hick, 'Rational Theistic Belief without Proofs' in Badham (ed.), *A John Hick Reader*, 59.

Hick's apparent commitment to scepticism is not one that would
have been shared by Jesus and others of great conviction. Nonetheless, perhaps Hick is able to make a special case for the great saints
and yet claim that ordinary religious believers should share his sceptic faith. How compelling are the grounds of ordinary believers'
faith?

Reasons for Belief

Running through Hick's work is the idea that the rationality of theistic faith is justified on the grounds of vivid religious experience. It
follows from this that not everyone would be justified in holding
theism to be true: only those whose experience leads them to
believe in some kind of transcendent reality. In his contribution to
Arguments for the Existence of God Hick observes that religious belief
does not normally arise from speculative logical arguments or
proofs: 'The claims of religion are claims made by individuals and
communities on the basis of their experience'.[30] Therefore, it would
be unfair to test the rationality of someone's belief on the basis of
proofs or logical reasons. Rather, the appropriate test would be
whether the experience of believers is strong enough for them to be
rationally justified in believing what they do. Clearly, most people
do not claim the kind of vivid, unrelenting religious experience
attributed to Jesus. Therefore, how much can ordinary believers be
justified in basing their religious outlook on their experience?

Hick deploys a form of the parity argument (an argument from
analogy) in order to justify such ordinary belief. The analogy he
makes is between ordinary sense experience and religious experience. After all, the sceptic tradition both undermined certainty over
the truth of sense experience and yet recommended living on the
assumption that sense experience is veridical. Hick follows the
work of a later sceptic, David Hume, in accepting that there is no
theoretical guarantee that sense experience is trustworthy. Hick
points out that this follows the 'success of Hume's attempt to show
that our normal non-solipsist belief in an objective world of endur-
ing objects around us in space is neither a product of, nor justifiable

---

[30] Hick, 'Rational', 55.

by, philosophical reasoning but is what has been called . . . a natural belief'.[31]

Hume's work also shares many similarities with the sceptic tradition. He offers various sceptic arguments against the trustworthiness of sense experience, only then to transcend them with his notion of natural belief.[32] Hick also appeals to natural belief in order to transcend sceptical conclusions.

A 'natural belief' is a kind of belief that has no final theoretical justification but is still essential and natural to human existence. It is a kind of common-sense belief that we all share, living as if it were true even though we might not be able to prove its truth. One simply cannot live without assuming that there really is an objective universe despite the difficulty of rationally proving such an assumption. The answer, in the tradition of the sceptics, is to admit the limitations of theoretical knowledge and accept the cultural norms or common sense of our culture as natural beliefs.

Hick points out two features of sense experience that induce trust in its veridical nature. The first is the involuntary character of such experience – it is so compelling that one feels unable, psychologically, to believe otherwise. The second feature is the practical advantage one finds in living on the assumption that the experience is veridical. Living as if our sense experience is normally accurate enables us to 'act successfully'[33] in the world. Taken together, these two features provide ample reason for people to trust their basic sense experience of the world. For Hick, such belief is justified belief even without any convincing, logical arguments. He then applies the same argument for belief in the religious significance of the universe.

Religious experience is, for many, of a sufficiently compelling quality that it would seem reasonable to trust its reliability. If the experience is significantly compelling, then it would seem insane for those who have such an experience to do otherwise: 'he is no more inclined to doubt its veridical character than to doubt the evidence of his senses'.[34] Thus there is an analogy between the insanity

---

[31] Hick, 'Rational', 57.
[32] For the distinction between Hume and classical scepticism see Helm, *Belief Policies*, 159–63.
[33] Hick, 'Rational', 58.
[34] Hick, 'Rational', 59.

of not trusting in sense experience and a kind of insanity, for some religious believers, in their not trusting their own religious experience. If natural belief is justified then, according to the parity argument, so is religious belief.

Credulous Belief

In *An Interpretation of Religion* Hick incorporates the principle of credulity into his account.[35] This principle claims that, given no obvious countervailing considerations, one should trust that how one perceives things to be is how things really are. Countervailing considerations might include the amount of alcohol recently consumed, the effects of drugs, or the brevity of an experience. If such countervailing considerations are not present, then, according to the principle of credulity, not to trust our basic perceptions of the world as an external reality would be insane. Now as we have seen in the case of Christ, alongside whom Hick places many great religious leaders from various traditions, experience of a transcendent reality was just as compelling as any natural beliefs. Therefore, according to the principle of credulity, it would be madness (literally) for such a holy person not to believe in a divine reality.

However, Hick assumes that probably none of his readership has the intensity of experience that marks these great saints. The rationality of belief in the case of exceptional experience provides only a weak foundation for rationality in the case of ordinary, fleeting religious experience. Therefore, while the parity argument may easily work in the case of Jesus or the Buddha, it does not so easily work for the ordinary believer. For this reason, Hick provides a discussion of how an ordinary believer's faith may be justified.

Hick acknowledges that anyone who does not have compelling religious experience 'cannot have the same justification for belief as those who do'.[36] He discusses the justification of belief in the case of two different kinds of ordinary believers. Firstly, there are those who have no religious experience of any significance. 'They might

---

[35] The principle is developed in Swinburne, *The Existence of God*.
[36] Hick, *Interpretation*, 221.

possibly . . . be so impressed by the moral and spiritual fruits of faith in the lives of the saints as to be drawn to share, at least tentatively, the latter's beliefs – in which case it would . . . be proper to count their being impressed in this way as itself a secondary kind of religious experience.'[37]

The second kind of person is in a similar, once removed, position as far as vivid religious experience is concerned. He or she does have religious experience, but it is less intense, a 'remote echo',[38] of the kind of experience described by those great saints. These remote echoes come in the form of occasional peak experiences of the divine presence during moments of heightened awareness. Because such beliefs are more sporadic and less compelling than those of the great saints, 'One's belief is not so deeply or solidly grounded as theirs.'[39] Even though these grounds for belief are not as solid, they still provide enough grounds for religious belief to be justified.

In each of these ways the justification of belief always comes down to some form of religious experience. Putting them together, there are essentially three levels of such experience related to each other in a similar way to the three steps in Hick's epistemology. The first is *being impressed by the claims of someone else or stories about them*. This form of religious experience provides grounds for faith, but they are weak and 'always vulnerable to the kind of sceptical challenge' found in the modern world.[40] The second level is *momentary peak experiences* that give further cause to trust in the validity of deeper experiences others claim to have had. In this case, personal experience bolsters the confidence one has in the more profound experience spoken of by someone else. The third, highest, level is that of *the great saints themselves*, whose religious experience is continuous with their experience of the natural world. While each level varies in the extent to which it provides grounds for the reasonableness of belief, nonetheless each does provide enough grounds for belief to be justified at least for that believer. Hick rests his case for the rationality of faith on the personal experience of the believer. Whatever the intensity, faith is justified by experience.

---

[37] Hick, *Interpretation*, 221.

[38] Hick, *Interpretation*, 222.

[39] Hick, *Interpretation*, 223.

[40] Hick, *Interpretation*, 222.

Hick places great weight on the evidential value of religious belief, and has done so throughout his work. It is a continuous thread running through both his early philosophical work and his later developments of the pluralist hypothesis. It is compatible with both the more orthodox Christianity of his early work and the radical theology of his later work because of two relevant features.

Firstly, Hick's description of religious experience is *individualistic*. Neither traditions nor religions as a whole are the subjects of justification: the personal, or even private, religious feelings of individuals are. Therefore, if a prima facie similarity of experience can be seen among individuals throughout the world religions, then Hick is happy to marginalise the significance of the traditions to which those individuals belong. What matters to his argument is the quality or intensity of personal experience, not the religious structures in which it happened to have taken place.

Secondly, Hick's account of religious experience has *minimal content*. It is largely an account of a quality of experience rather than an account of the content of experience. His use of such expressions as the 'divine presence' or 'limitless goodness' to identify the content of religious experience is deliberately vague. So little can be expressly said regarding the content of religious experience that Hick is easily able to extend his epistemology from the Christian tradition to incorporate any of the major world religions.

We have now established Hick's basic theory of knowledge, the aspect of his work that lends continuity to his thought as a whole. Indeed, right from the outset, his theories seem to be remarkably compatible with the pluralist outlook. Though Hick would not describe himself as a sceptic, his system fits well with this school of thought. It is a system of thought that denies any grounds for certainty in matters of ultimate belief. The only basis for such convictions lies in the personal intensity of our experience regarding divine reality. While these may not impress anyone else they do provide a basis for our own personal choice of a religious outlook. However, such experiences do not provide grounds for a whole doctrinal pattern of belief. In keeping with scepticism, Hick urges us to draw a distinction between the way things appear to us and the way they really are. As we shall discuss further, Hick's sympathies lie with the German philosopher Immanuel Kant. Interestingly, it was Kant who set himself the task of answering the sceptic challenge posed by Hume and providing justification for practical religion even without proofs for the truth of theism. In the next chapter we shall explore the connection to Kant's theology in more detail as the background to Hick's pluralist hypothesis. This will open up a perspective on where we should place Hick's approach to religion in the history of western thought. In so doing, we shall have a stronger position from which to assess the pluralist case.

Chapter 5

The Kantian Heritage

Kant's philosophy has always exercised a degree of influence on Hick's thought, though this influence has become more prominent in his most recent work. In this chapter and the next we shall trace his use of Kant and analyse the implications of drawing upon Kant's epistemology for understanding religion. We shall begin by assessing Hick's direct and indirect appropriation of Kant's work, and then examine the continuity between these two thinkers. This continuity is much greater than Hick acknowledges. He dismisses such criticism with defences like, 'I have only borrowed from Kant his basic noumenal/phenomenal distinction, and am well aware that his own epistemology of religion is very different from that which I am recommending.'[1] While I acknowledge that Hick is only explicitly borrowing a limited Kantian insight, the implicit debt the pluralist hypothesis owes to Kant is remarkable – a claim I shall try to demonstrate.

The connection between Hick's pluralist hypothesis and a Kantian view of religion allows us to place Hick in a particular western tradition of thought. We find the roots of pluralism in a tradition of scepticism running from the Pyrronian sceptics of ancient Greece, through David Hume and Immanuel Kant, finding expression in the entire modernist approach to religion. This is not, of course, a book about Kant, and my exposition is necessarily limited to a few key factors that shed light on the pluralist hypothesis.

---

[1] Hick, 'Ineffability', 46.

Hick's Debt to Kant

In his early work, Hick rejected Kant's claim that God and immortality were only postulates of reason. Hick prefered to establish them as postulates of experience. He distanced himself from the intellectualism of Kant: 'For the purpose of our inquiry, the main comment to be made upon this Kantian theory is that it leaves no room for any acquaintance with or experience of the divine, such as religious persons claim.'[2]

As we have already noted, Hick understands religious belief to be justified by a believer's personal religious faith. God, therefore, is not a postulate of reason or morality but is a felt presence. Nonetheless, in Hick's later work he acknowledges a limited validity in Kant's approach. Regarding the demands of morality, Hick shares Kant's conviction that such demands presuppose the existence of a higher reality: 'To recognise moral claims as taking precedence over all other interests is, implicitly, to believe in a reality of some kind, other than the natural world, that is superior to oneself and entitled to one's obedience.'[3]

Hick shares with Kant the claim that the existence of God is indirectly justified by moral belief. Of course, for Hick moral claims are only the second step in his epistemology. The third step, that of religious experience, provides more direct justification. Indeed, Hick argues that this is a consistent addition that may be made to Kant's thought and one with which Kant may not have been displeased. Hick believes Kant was developing his thought in a direction that would have brought him closer to his own epistemology of religion: 'in the later very fragmentary *Opus Postumum* Kant moved toward a different view according to which the experience of the moral law, instead of being treated as the basis for a theistic postulation, is thought of as in some manner mediating the divine presence and will'.[4]

---

[2] Hick, *Faith and Knowledge*, 62.

[3] Hick, *Philosophy of Religion*, 29.

[4] Hick, *Faith*, 63. Despite what Hick takes as hopeful signs in Kant's later work, Michalson points out that the *Opus Postumum* denies the existence of God as a personal being independent of human moral experience; *Kant and the Problem of God*, 32–3.

Such a movement in Kant's thought would have brought his epistemology to a position much closer to that reached by Hick. The description of God as postulate may be intellectually satisfying, but it is very unsatisfactory as an account of the religious experience of believers. Hick finds little indication that Kant took such experience seriously. Yet this modification of his thought could have led Kant to a more sympathetic interpretation of religious belief.

There is a great deal in Kant's moral thought that Hick is concerned to affirm. This is particularly so with reference to Kant's 'categorical imperative' which Hick describes as a high point of his thought. Hick claims that in the imperative Kant has given philosophical expression to Christ's golden rule.[5] Kant used the 'categorical imperative' as a way of defining ethics as legitimate for their own sake: they do not need to be justified with reference to anything else. Hick describes this approach to morality as one compatible with both Christianity and Buddhism. Kant's 'man of duty' who does things with no thought of personal reward is equivalent to the *arhat* of eastern thought. Hick describes Kant's ethics as 'a useful stepping-stone to the more positive and mysterious things that are said about nirvana in the pali canon'.[6] Hick finds Kant so helpful on this point because morality is defined in quite neutral terms that may be seen as compatible with any religious tradition. True moral behaviour gives no thought to consequences and is done unconditionally, and this theoretical exposition of the core of moral belief requires no particular religious framework.

But the most sustained use Hick makes of Kant is with regard to his epistemology. In particular, Kant's thought helps Hick to modify his own earlier statement of epistemology and to bring it into line with his pluralist hypothesis. The three-step theory of interpretation is compatible with the pluralist hypothesis that there are many different interpretations of the same religious object. However, Hick's early statement of this theory does not explain *why* there should be such varied interpretations. This is particularly significant given that there is not great variety in the first two steps of natural or moral interpretation. For example, across the world today

---

[5] Hick, *Death and Eternal Life*, 426.
[6] Hick, *Death*, 435.

there is substantial agreement on the basic fruitfulness of the scientific method. This presses the question as to why there should be such variation in religious belief. In his early work, Hick's stress on cognitive freedom was primarily used to explain the freedom to choose between a naturalistic or theistic interpretation. It did not explain why there should be so many different non-naturalistic interpretations – the world does not simply divide into Christians and atheists, but into Christians, atheists, Jews, Muslims, Hindus and endless varieties of each. Hick draws directly from Kant's epistemology in order to explain such pluralism.

The basic thesis of Hick's later statement of religious knowledge relies upon the crucial distinction between 'the Real *an sich* and the Real as variously experienced-and-thought by different human communities'.[7] Human communities do not perceive the Real as it is. Their perception is always conditioned by the cultural context in which it occurs. Therefore, the Real as perceived is not the same as the Real that is not perceived. A theoretical framework for this claim is provided by 'one of Kant's most basic epistemological insights', which Hick expresses in general terms as: 'the mind actively interprets sensory information in terms of concepts, so that the environment as we consciously perceive and inhabit it is our familiar three-dimensional world of objects interacting in space'.[8]

The familiar environment we think we inhabit is the real world as it really is. There is an active component in human knowledge – the mind does not passively receive sensory information from which to construct a view of the world. The empiricist thinker John Locke expressed such an idea, describing the mind as 'white paper void of all characters' until written upon with ideas from experience.[9] Nor is the environment the construction of the mind alone, as if the world were nothing more than ideas. Rationalist philosophers proposed this latter notion. Kant affirms a combination of both sensory information and the active role of the mind in contributing to the creation of that information. The characteristics of dimensional experience – time, space, substance, causality and so on – are all categories of the mind through which otherwise chaotic

---

[7] Hick, *An Interpretation of Religion*, 236.

[8] Hick, *Interpretation*, 240.

[9] Locke, *An Essay Concerning Human Understanding*, 33.

sensory information is ordered and given meaning for us. Hick is well aware that this is but one, simple, aspect of Kant's thought. He freely admits that his own application of Kantian thought is not one of which the philosopher himself would necessarily have approved. Indeed, Hick claims that the basic thrust of Kant's principle not only arises from late western thought but may also be discerned in the work of Thomas Aquinas and the Muslim theologian Al Junaid.[10] However, it would be misleading to think that Hick is merely drawing upon Kant for illustrative material. He is adopting a specifically Kantian insight. The specific insight is Kant's distinction 'between an entity as it is in itself and as it appears in perception'.[11] This distinction is characterised as *noumenon* and *phenomenon* (see Chapter 2) where the latter indicates reality as ordered by our interpretative activity and the former indicates the world as it is in itself.

The Pluralist Modification of Kant

This basic Kantian insight must be modified in order to suit the pluralist hypothesis. Hick is not concerned with applying this insight to the level of natural belief, as Kant would certainly have done, but to the third step: religious belief. This is the stage of epistemology that permits the greatest freedom for what men and women may believe. The Kantian framework helps to explain why there should be such diversity among the world religions.

Hick is using Kant's insight in an analogous sense to describe the Ultimate Reality behind religious belief as the *noumenon* and the actual beliefs of religious people as the *phenomenon*. Hick accepts that in making this application, his work departs from that of Kant. In particular, Kant's God is a postulate of morality, whereas for Hick religious experience in all its forms assumes some kind of divine reality.

> But for Kant God is postulated, not experienced. In partial agreement but also partial disagreement with him, I want to say that the Real *an sich* is postulated by us as a pre-supposition, not of the moral life, but of

---

[10] Hick, *Interpretation*, 241.
[11] Hick, *Interpretation*, 241.

religious experience and the religious life, whilst the gods, as also the mystically known Brahman, Sunyata and so on, are phenomenal manifestations of the Real occurring within the realm of religious experience.[12]

Hick affirms the existence of God (or the Real) in the same way Kant affirmed the noumenon: it is the ground of phenomena; and its existence explains the way things appear. Just as Kant took the appearance of reality as an indicator that there is such a thing as reality, so Hick understands the appearance of God in the world religions. There must be something behind those appearances. We may note here how close Kant and Hick (at least in his later work) are, despite differences over how to apply this kind of epistemology. For both Kant and the later Hick, the noumenon is only a postulate of human knowledge; it is not something we can have direct access to. This point is not always evident when Hick's work is understood as a coherent whole, because, in his earlier accounts, he was more comfortable describing a mediated experience of the Real.[13] But, in keeping with a Kantian epistemology, there is no such mediation. Our experience is only ever an experience of phenomena. Noumenon is not something we indirectly experience, but only something we may postulate. Therefore, 'When we speak of a moral God . . . we are speaking of the Real as humanly experienced: that is, as phenomenon.'[14] Hick describes images like 'Creator God' or 'Heavenly Father' as the persona of the Real. It is this persona that is the object of experience, not the Real itself. The sharpness of this distinction is highly significant and must be borne in mind in any interpretation of Hick's work.

The Real is not something men and women ever experience. It is something postulated as the necessary explanation for religious experience. Despite Hick's own claims, it seems clear that the noumenal Reality is just as much (and as little) a postulate for Hick as it was for Kant. The only real difference between them on this point is that Kant describes God as a postulate of morality rather than of religious experience. However, even this difference is not as

---

[12] Hick, *Interpretation*, 243.

[13] E.g. Hick, *Faith*, 63.

[14] Hick, *Interpretation*, 246.

significant as it may at first appear. As we have seen with Hick's three-step epistemology, religious experience is essentially moralistic: it includes, while transcending, the second step of moral interpretation. Religious experience is a kind of deeper appreciation of moral experience rather than something wholly other. Thus, in a very real sense, Hick adds little to Kant's view of God as postulate of morality.

The central theme that unites Hick to a Kantian epistemology is the absolute divide between the Real *an sich* and the Real as experienced. For Hick this theme is particularly useful as it both explains why there should be a diversity of religions (there being no direct access to divine reality) and why religious people ought to value that diversity (there being no way of settling such differences). In a moment we shall see why this outlook is problematic, but for now let us consider a little further Kant's own expression of the phenomenon–noumenon relationship.

Cause and Effect

Kant, who had been greatly occupied with the ideas of David Hume, was party to the mainstream of German rationalist philosophy until, in his famous words, the work of Hume 'interrupted my dogmatic slumber'.[15] Hume's treatment of causality had brought to the surface a fundamental problem in epistemology. An example of what we might call 'causality' is the relationship between a flame and its heat upon us. Hume describes the relationship in a way that raises the basic epistemic problem: 'Thus we remember to have seen that species of object we call *flame*, and to have felt that species of sensation we call *heat*. We likewise call to mind their constant conjunction in all past instances. Without any farther ceremony, we call the one *cause*, and the other *effect*, and infer the existence of the one from that of the other.'[16]

What Hume describes as an absence of ceremony is also an absence of experimental evidence. There is no thing, 'causation', that we have identified in this process of connecting heat to flame –

---

[15] Kant, *Prolegomena*, 7.
[16] Hume, *A Treatise of Human Nature*, 61.

all that has been described is the constant conjunction of events and the natural habit of relating them to one another through the concept of cause and effect. Hume applied this kind of analysis to many areas of thought and exposed the weakness of empiricism. Many of our most treasured beliefs are not based upon sensory evidence or experience, as the empiricists thought, but rather on simple habits of mind. Exactly what Hume wanted to make of these startling conclusions is the subject of debate. A mainstream view of his work describes him as a sceptic. Bertrand Russell accuses Hume of a kind of scepticism that represented the 'bankruptcy of eighteenth-century reasonableness'.[17] Hume certainly gave good reason for this interpretation. For example, he claimed that 'sceptical doubt arises naturally from a profound and intense reflection on those subjects, it always increases, the farther we carry our reflections' such that 'Carelesseness and in-attention alone can afford us any remedy.'[18]

Norman Kemp Smith, another influence on Hick, broke the long tradition of interpreting Hume as a sceptic and, instead, emphasised the place of natural instinctual belief as the grounds of knowledge.[19] Hume's scepticism was more a methodological ploy to demonstrate the significance of the common-sense habits of our mind. The significance of such common sense is rather lost sight of in the schools of empiricist and rationalist philosophy, but Hume established afresh the significance of natural belief.

Kant understood the sceptical challenge posed by Hume's work and set himself the task of establishing new foundations for knowledge. Following Hume, Kant accepted the a priori status of many beliefs (such as causation) and sought to show how a coherent epistemology could proceed on this basis. Hume had merely set the problem for which Kant was providing the solution. Kant contrasted his work with that of Hume, who 'ran his ship ashore, for safety's sake, landing on scepticism, there to let it lie and rot; whereas my object is rather to give it a pilot, who, by means of safe astronomical principles . . . may steer the ship safely'.[20]

---

[17] Russell, *A History of Western Philosophy*, 645.

[18] Hume, *Treatise*, 144.

[19] Kemp Smith, *The Philosophy of David Hume*.

[20] Kant, *Prolegomena*, 9. The boat metaphor is also used by Hume (*Treatise*, 171–2).

In his response to Hume's scepticism, Kant maintained that the mind was formed by a priori intuitions. For example, the notions or categories of space and time are intuitions of the human mind already present when we encounter reality. Therefore, all reality must be ordered by the mind in terms of spatial position (space) and temporal sequence (time). Knowledge is simply impossible without the a priori contribution of these intuitions. Kant drew up a table of the concepts of the human mind, which provided a kind of framework in which all our experience occurs. Kant's solution to Hume's scepticism was to affirm the subjective contribution of the human mind to knowledge, while also establishing empirical realism on the basis that human knowledge presupposes the reality of an external world. Thus we arrive at the distinction between our knowledge of reality and the way things really are. If we are to know anything at all, then certain subjective concepts must be applied to our immediate sensations: 'concepts which have their origin quite *a priori* in the pure understanding, and under which every perception must first of all be subsumed and then their means changed into experience'.[21]

Thus far, we may readily identify Hick's use of Kant's categories and intuitions as analogous to the role of religion and doctrine, where human thought forms shape religious experience into its culturally peculiar forms. This is a kind of analogous use of Kant's insights made by Hick. After all, in contrast to the role of Kant's categories, doctrinal or religious beliefs may be adopted for a variety of reasons, be dropped or changed as time goes by, and be held with varying degrees of strength and conviction. Kant's a priori categories do not have these features because they are prior to and not dependent on experience. However useful Kant's work may be as a picture of how religion functions, this is clearly an analogous use rather than a direct application of his work. A more direct dependence on Kant is evident in the way both thinkers assume a form of dualism.

Dualism is suggested by the sharp divide between the phenomenal world, ordered and comprehended by the active participation of the mind, and the noumenon beyond comprehension. In the *Critique of Pure Reason* Kant sheds further light on the limits of human

---

[21] Kant, *Prolegomena*, 54–5.

knowledge. Here he considers the possibility that there might be some form of sixth sense, perhaps a mystic sense of the noumenon, which would provide knowledge by acquaintance. If this were possible, then it would be a positive sense of the noumenon as 'an object of a non-sensible intuition'.[22] However, Kant's epistemology rules out such a possibility. All objects arise with sense experience, and as experience is necessarily shaped by the mind no direct acquaintance is possible. We have

> no intuition, indeed not even the concept of a possible intuition, through which objects outside of the field of sensibility could be given, and about which the understanding could be employed *assertorically*. The concept of a noumenon is therefore merely a *boundary concept*, in order to limit the pretension of sensibility, and therefore only of negative use.[23]

It follows from this argument that the only things we can say about the noumenon are negative claims. We cannot say anything positive (assertorically) about what the noumenon is. In effect, the noumenon is simply a limiting concept. It does rule out the solipsistic claim that there is nothing beyond the figments of our imagination. Clearly there is something there. Kant refuses the path of non-realism in his epistemology, but is agnostic about what the 'something' actually is. Whatever noumena are, the understanding 'sets boundaries for itself, not cognizing these things through categories, hence merely thinking them under the name of an unknown something'.[24] In this sense, we may describe Kant's position as agnostic. Of course, what Kant means by 'noumenon' is not God, or even Hick's divine being, but all of reality considered in itself. Nonetheless, Kant's agnosticism regarding reality emerges as a theological agnosticism in Hick's work.

Kant's epistemology may be characterised as being founded upon a picture of two worlds of truth. One world is accessible and dependent upon the active participation of the mind, whereas the other world of truth is simply a regulative, limiting concept about which little can be said. It is a necessary postulate of empirical realism, but

---

[22] Kant, *Critique of Pure Reason*, 347.

[23] Kant, *Critique*, 350.

[24] Kant, *Critique*, 351.

not a subject for assertive propositions. Hick's pluralist thesis makes good use of this two-worlds view of truth: a shared noumenal reality is the postulate of the plural phenomena worshipped, adored or revered by the adherents of various religious traditions. Such an analysis has great explanatory power. However, there are two related difficulties for this application of Kant's analysis.

Firstly, there is concern over the legitimacy of Hick's reading of Kant. Terry F. Godlove makes a significant critique of Hick's use of Kant by pointing out that a plurality of conceptual schemes is incompatible with Kant's epistemology.[25] He points out the universality of the Kantian categories – all people share them. The universality of the categories is demonstrated by the broadly common view of reality held by all people, at all times, throughout the world. While this feature of Kant is passed over by Hick who wants to allow space for a diversity of interpretations, this difficulty need not detain us here as Hick himself admits that his use of Kant involves modification for his own purposes. Even if he has misunderstood Kant in an important way, that is not fatal for his argument. However, the second difficulty is more serious. The implications of dualism in Kant's work have raised serious problems and these must also be directed at the work of Hick.

Kant's epistemology has been subjected to much discussion and diverse interpretation, but we shall identify just one particular issue: how far one can square two worlds of truth with a critical-realist epistemology. How can we really be sure that our language identifies something that is really 'there' and not just in the mind? Let us see how this charge may be levelled at Kant.

The Grounds of Realism

One may question the compatibility of Kant's thought with his cognitive realism. The fundamental problem is that the notion of objectivity itself cannot be known through experience and so must be a construction of the mind. This inevitably leads to a radical prob-

---

[25] Godlove, *Religion, Interpretation, and Diversity of Belief*. Godlove suggests Hick's reading is dependent on a misunderstanding of Kant introduced into religious studies by Emile Durkheim.

lem for realism. There is nothing of any significance that we can say about the noumenon – not even that it exists. Kant describes the realm beyond appearances as 'empty (for us)',[26] as entirely abstract and unknowable. There is nothing that can be said about it. Kant wants simultaneously to hold that there is something there and that we can say nothing about it. However, the thing-in-itself, when abstracted so completely from the possibilities of perceptual knowledge, loses meaning and content. Its function is then merely a sop to realism, which Kant made in order to distance himself from solipsism or idealism. Therefore, what would be at stake in abandoning the notion altogether and turning instead to radical non-realism? In the area of philosophy there is an example of just such an approach in the work of Richard Rorty. In the area of theology one might give the example of Don Cupitt. Hick has remained a critic of Cupitt and is sensitive to the charge that he might be guilty of the same non-realist framework. Though Hick denies it, the implications of Kantianism certainly suggest the charge.

George Schrader made the insightful suggestion that Kant is inconsistent in his epistemology because of two rival forces at work in his thought. On the one hand, there is the critical position that he develops in his three critiques. However, on the other hand, there is also his pre-critical commitment to God and pietism. According to Schrader this pre-critical outlook constantly bedevilled his philosophy.[27] These two forces give rise to a basic inconsistency in Kant's work. In order to establish realism he must apply the categories of pure reason beyond their proper boundaries so that they tell us something about the noumenon. 'One may posit the thing-in-itself as the cause of appearances which are known, but then one is guilty of extending the category of causality beyond the realm of appearances, a procedure which [Kant] had explicitly repudiated.'[28]

---

[26] Kant, *Critique*, 350.

[27] Others see these commitments as belonging together such that Kant is truly an orthodox Christian philosopher. Westphal argues that Kant's theism is so important in all his thought that the thing-in-itself is only properly understood as the thing-for-God; 'In Defence of the Thing in Itself', 119. This argument is plausible but I do not find it convincing.

[28] Schrader, 'The Thing in Itself in Kantian Philosophy' in Wolff (ed.), *Kant: A Collection of Critical Essays*, 172.

It is absolutely inconsistent to claim that the noumenon is the cause of the phenomenal world when causality has already been established as a category of the mind, and not something that belongs to the thing-in-itself. In what sense could the noumenon be said to 'cause' something if this category cannot be applied to things in themselves? Schrader argues that 'while Kant flatly declared that reality in itself is theoretically unknowable, he could not escape trying to formulate meaningful theoretical concepts of it'.[29] Nicholas Rescher attributes the inconsistency to a looseness in the way Kant formulates his thought on this issue. Rescher distinguishes two forms of causality. On the one hand, there is *'authentic causality*, which is genuinely experientiable' and, on the other hand, *'generic grounding*, which is merely intelligible'.[30] According to this distinction Kant did not mean to imply an authentic causal relationship between noumenon and phenomenon. Thus when Kant speaks of one 'affecting' the other he does not mean this in causal terms. Instead, it is a principle of 'Sufficient Reason' that 'controls what we must think to be the case, rather than what we can claim to know regarding nature'.[31] This argument is unconvincing and simply relies on equivocation over what, exactly, is meant by a term like 'affecting'. Nonethless, Rescher salvages Kant's position at a price. The price of denying a causal connection between noumenon and phenomenon is a radical dualism, and the dualism implicit in Kantian thought leads inexorably from agnosticism to atheism. We are not really able to say anything about reality beyond appearances. All these problems haunt Hick's own epistemology.

William L. Rowe applies these problems to Hick's own distinction between the Real as noumenon and religious beliefs as phenomena. He asks what remaining ontological status can be claimed for phenomenal descriptions of the deity. Do they describe something that really exists? His answer points ahead to a conclusion Hick would not want to admit: 'Although Hick does not commit himself, I suspect that he thinks of them as analogous to "veridical hallucinations" – no such entities really exist, but these "appearances" are occasions of a salvation/liberation process in

---

[29] Schrader, 'Thing in Itself', 188.
[30] Rescher, *Kant and the Reach of Reason*, 23.
[31] Rescher, *Kant*, 34.

which human beings are transformed from self-centred to real-
ity-centred beings.'[32]

To be consistent with Kant's thought, phenomena cannot be
described as 'real' because they are only ever constructions of the
mind made in response to an unknown (and unknowable) reality.
Thus Rowe is entirely consistent to describe Hick's phenomena as
non-existent. Hick, to be consistent, should deny the actual *existence* of God, Christ, Allah, Brahman, and so on. All he may
consistently do is to postulate a Real about which nothing can be
said as a way of explaining our veridical hallucinations. To push the
problem further, Schrader following, we must also point out that no
causal connection can be maintained between the Real and the
appearances perceived by the categories of understanding. Causation is a category of the mind and not something we can ascribe to
the noumenon. This leads to a radical non-realism. We can learn
nothing about the noumenon from phenomenal appearances,
because the category of causation is not open to us. The Real cannot be meaningfully described as 'existing' or 'causing', because we
have no epistemic grounds to apply such terms beyond phenomena.
Hick's adoption of a Kantian epistemology involves an implicit
rejection of religious realism.[33] George Michalson's critique of Kant
on this point applies very readily to Hick:

> [A] sudden reversion to the idea that God is the ground of the highest
> original good hardly mitigates the speculative difficulties he has intro-
> duced with these considerations. Certainly Kant cannot assume the re-
> lation between the world and God that animates the cosmological
> proof, even apart from his criticism of the proof itself. For he has
> himself eliminated the role of causality in this relation through his tran-
> scendental turn.[34]

Kant's use of the term 'ground', given the impossibility of causation, has only rhetorical force in his argument. This same problem

---

[32] Rowe, 'John Hick's Contribution to the Philosophy of Religion' in
Sharma (ed.), *God, Truth and Reality: Essays in Honour of John Hick*, 22.
[33] A point made by Eddy, 'John Hick's Theological Pilgrimage' in *Proceedings of the Wheaton Theology Conference*.
[34] Michalson, *Kant*, 53.

besets Hick's work. Given an absolute distinction between the categories of the mind and Ultimate Reality there is a significant problem in claiming anything whatsoever about the Real.

Hick and the Real

If Kant's distinction between noumena and phenomena was difficult enough for himself to sustain, it certainly runs into similar problems in the work of Hick. If the Real is truly and strictly beyond the categories provided by religion and culture, then nothing can be said of it and, as a result, it can only be a 'nothing' of which not even existence can be predicated. Furthermore, not only are the objects of religious devotion to be distinguished from the Real in-itself, but there is also no way of making any connection between those objects and the Real. Hick often uses the expression 'manifestations of the Real' to describe the connection between the Real and phenomena but, owing to his underlying epistemology, the word 'manifestation' is emptied of force. Normally manifestation implies causation but causality is a category of the mind and not applicable to the thing-in-itself. This problem is particularly acute given Hick's dismissal of the possibility of revelation. Revelation is dismissed and yet retained at least in some implicit sense in a word like 'manifestation'. (We shall deal with the problem of revelation in chapter 9.)

Hick responds to such criticisms by maintaining that while our concepts or doctrines do not apply to the Real, we may 'make certain purely formal statements about the postulated Real'.[35] Hick wishes to distinguish between formal and substantive claims about God, and must do this in order to sustain the pluralist hypothesis. As Christopher Insole has argued, the distinction is incoherent.[36] Formal claims regarding God are dependent upon substantive claims. If we have no certain substantial knowledge of God, then it is simply not possible to establish the logical, formal claims we might wish to

---

[35] Hick, *Interpretation*, 246.
[36] Insole, 'Why John Hick Cannot, and Should Not, Stay out of the Jam Pot', 27–30.

make. Nonetheless, Hick claims to identify two such formal statements that provide important information about the Real. Following Anselm, Hick affirms that the Real is 'that than which no greater can be conceived', and, following Kant, that the Real is 'the noumenal ground of the encountered gods'.[37] These formal statements look encouraging as a basis on which to build a realist view of religious language. However, in the light of a Kantian epistemology, it is not easy to see what content these statements have. In the latter statement it is difficult to substantiate what Hick might mean by 'ground'. It seems most likely that Hick means that something like a causal connection exists between the noumenal reality and the way gods appear to us. However, this would suffer all the problems of applying causation beyond appearances that we have already noted. The meaning of the former statement is much more limited in Hick's work than in the tradition of Anselm. It is only a limiting notion for Hick: nothing greater than the Real can be conceived because the Real itself cannot be conceived. One could equally well postulate that the Real is 'that than which nothing less can be conceived' for all its cognitive value. The word 'greater' has no theological significance for Hick, but simply pays lip-service to Anselm's theological position. Anselm clearly did intend something substantive by his use of the word 'greater'. For example, in his response to Gaunilo he writes, 'For we attribute to the divine substance anything of which it can be conceived that it is better to be than not to be that thing. For example: it is better to be eternal, than not eternal; good, than not good; nay, goodness itself, than not goodness itself.'[38]

By 'greater' Anselm sought to relate God to His self-revelation as good, eternal, and as a God who exists. Such specific terms are not open to Hick for whom such language would represent an illicit bridge between the Real and its phenomenal manifestations. Hick only uses Anselm's language to point out that the noumenon is beyond, greater than all conception. Such an empty notion shares absolutely nothing in common with Anselm's deeply theistic onto-

---

[37] Hick, *Interpretation*, 246.
[38] Anselm, 'St. Anselm's Reply to Gaunilo', in Plantinga (ed.), *The Ontological Argument*, 13–27.

logical argument. It is this kind of emptiness at the heart of Hick's concept of the Real that prompts Loughlin to point out that 'At the centre of Hick's universe of faiths there is an "empty space" ', which he likens to Barthes' Tokyo, a city which turns around a forbidden and empty centre.[39]

Hick makes eclectic use of his sources, and cannot thus be labelled as the follower of any one school of thought. Where helpful, he draws upon Kant or Wittgenstein or Hume or Ayer in order to advance his work. With reference to Kant, Hick acknowledges his debt to a basic epistemological insight, but distances himself from other features of his philosophy. However, a closer inspection of Kant's theological concerns reveals many more parallels with Hick's own work. We shall review Kant's theory of religion in a little detail in the next chapter so that this parallel can be seen. In doing so it must be emphasised that Hick himself does not explicitly acknowledge such parallels. Yet I think it can be easily shown that the mature statement Hick gives of his position is strikingly similar to that of Kant. Why should this be so? My suggestion is simple: a certain kind of epistemology, shared by Hick and Kant, will necessarily lead to a certain kind of theology. It is no accident that Kant provides an interpretation of religion similar to that which Hick arrives at by his own path, for both are driven by certain shared epistemological concerns.

---

[39] Loughlin, 'Noumenon and Phenomena', 505.

Chapter 6

Reasonable Religion

Kant's *Religion Within the Limits of Reason Alone* is often understood to be primarily concerned with ethics. Kant was a great moral philosopher who argued that morality could be understood and pursued outside any particular religious framework. However, Kant's treatment of ethics remains wedded to certain theological concerns: 'Morality thus leads ineluctably to religion, through which it extends itself to the idea of a powerful moral Lawgiver, outside of mankind, for Whose will that is the final end (of creation) which at the same time can and ought to be man's final end.'[1]

From the foundation of ethics Kant was led to consider the function of religion in human life. For him religion provided a motivation and vision for moral life, which he knew could not be provided by moral philosophy alone. Because of this background to his discussion of ethics, Kant's treatment of religion always emphasises morality. We can outline from his main work on religion four themes that find their echo in the work of Hick. These four themes are (1) freedom of the will, (2) the incarnation of Christ, (3) universal religion, and (4) the history of religion. We shall first survey these four themes in Kant's work and then describe the similar way in which Hick handles them.[2]

---

[1] Kant, *Religion Within the Limits of Reason Alone*, 5–6.
[2] In a personal communication Hick has told me that he last read Kant's *Religion* as a student and has not consciously been influenced by it. Needless to say, my argument is that Hick is led to a similar position because of his shared epistemology, rather than claiming that Hick directly borrows from Kant's theology.

Freedom of the Will

Because Kant is concerned to establish the validity of religion in
relation to morality he begins his account with a consideration of
the origins of evil and the freedom of the human will. Indeed, his
writing on religion is deeply concerned with theodicy. In keeping
with his philosophy, Kant argues that the origin of evil lies with the
exercise of free will: 'Man *himself* must make or have made himself
into whatever, in a moral sense, whether good or evil, he is or is to
become. Either condition must be an effect of his free choice; for
otherwise he could not be held responsible for it and could be *morally* neither good nor evil.'[3]

Created neutral, human beings have a freedom of will that entails
responsibility for choosing either good or evil. Kant's position is
opposed to the Augustinian or Calvinist emphasis on the bondage
of the will to sin and the consequent inability to choose the good
without the intervention of grace. In the apostle Paul's letter to the
Romans we read, 'So then he has mercy on whomever he chooses,
and he hardens the heart of whomever he chooses' (Rom. 9:18).
Commenting on this verse Calvin affirms that Paul 'teaches that salvation is prepared for those only on whom the Lord is pleased to
bestow mercy – that ruin and death await all whom he has not chosen'.[4] Kant cites the same verse but refuses to take it so literally.
Indeed, he comments that such teaching, 'taken according to the
letter, is the *salto mortale* of human reason'.[5] In contrast to Calvinism,
Kant stresses free will because in his system it is only because of their
free choice that individuals are held to be morally culpable for their
behaviour. Furthermore, because the choice to do what is good is
also utterly free and uncompelled, human beings are to be praised
for their right actions.

Kant was noted for reintroducing a doctrine of radical evil even
though the age in which he wrote had largely abandoned it. 'At a
time when leading Enlightenment thinkers were united in attacking ignorance as the source of evil, embodied especially in
outmoded traditions and superstitions, the aging Kant clearly argues

---

[3] Kant, *Religion*, 5–6.
[4] Calvin, *Institutes of the Christian Religion* 1.2, 289.
[5] Kant, *Religion*, 111.

that evil arises out of the will.'[6] Human beings are not inherently good creatures who, through right education, will inevitably choose the good. Nonetheless, Kant rejects such doctrines as the Calvinist understanding of original sin and total depravity with his higher view of human nature in which 'a seed of goodness still remains in its entire purity'.[7] There is no need for special grace or redemptive acts in order for men and women to choose the good. The seed of goodness remains intact and enables everyone to do good and, if they prefer to choose evil, to be morally culpable for their failure. Kant poses a simple but influential argument against Calvinist alternatives: 'For when the moral law commands that we *ought* now to be better men, it follows inevitably that we must *be able* to be better men.'[8] For actions to be genuinely moral they must be freely chosen. Mark Johnson describes Kant's treatment of freedom and morality in this way:

> [Kant] argues that morality cannot be based on God's will as the source of divine moral law, for that would reduce human freedom to a sham freedom to obey an 'other'. Yet he argues that morality *can* be based on universal law which we rationally give to ourselves . . . we are free just insofar as we are autonomous, that is, just to the extent that we give moral laws *to ourselves* of our rationality and freedom.[9]

Salvation is, then, the free pursuit of moral laws that we have autonomously chosen. What then of the historic Christian understanding of salvation as an act of God on our behalf? Kant uses the language of our having faith in the atonement but, as we shall see in a moment, the word 'atonement' is taken to be symbolic rather than literal. In contrast to the historic Christian position, Kant has no doubt that salvation is an active faith in the moral life, not faith in the validity of outdated doctrines: 'Where shall we start, i.e., with a faith in what God has done on our behalf, or with what we are to do to become worthy of God's assistance (whatever this may be)? In answering this question we cannot hesitate in deciding for the second alternative.'[10]

---

[6] Michalson, *Kant and the Problem of God*, 103–4.
[7] Kant, *Religion*, 41.
[8] Kant, *Religion*, 46.
[9] Johnson, *Moral Imagination*, 25.
[10] Kant, *Religion*, 108.

Saving faith is identified with our commitment to being morally pleasing to God. Religion, in its specific forms, is secondary to this moral faith. Belief in the atonement might be useful, but it does not take precedence over commitment to the moral imperatives of pure reason. Kant's treatment of Christianity provides some room for God to be active, but it is far from clear why that activity is, in any important sense, necessary.

This anthropology, with its emphasis on human free will, lays the foundation for Kant's reinterpretation of the meaning of Christianity. The extent to which it entails a radical reinterpretation is perhaps only seen with the benefit of centuries of hindsight. In surveying the subsequent history of thought we see that once this philosophical framework is adopted, the days of Christian theology are numbered. As Michalson writes in his survey of Kant's theology, 'with his aggressive account of autonomous rationality, Kant has cut off the head of the traditionally religious body, yet the corpse continues for a time to twitch and move, as though life is still in it when it is not'.[11] Though it looks as if Kant's theology remains Christian, the lifeblood, grace of God, has been drained away.

The Incarnation of Christ

The essence of religion, for Kant, is the moral law or imperative. In the light of this he interprets the significance of the historical peculiarities of Christianity. The incarnation is taken to be the personification of goodness, and so Jesus Christ is to be understood as the example, or archetype, of what all people are to be. However, the historical Jesus has only a contingent relationship to this archetype: 'We need therefore, no empirical example to make the idea of a person morally well-pleasing to God our archetype; this idea as an archetype is already present in our reason.'[12]

The historical Jesus is only a representation of the archetype which itself exists in each one of us and is accessible through the exercise of pure reason. In principle we need no knowledge of the historical Jesus or the gospel accounts in order to know what kind of people

---

[11] Michalson, *Kant*, 26.
[12] Kant, *Religion*, 56.

God calls us to be. Charlotte Allen notes that for Kant the future offered a time when 'Jesus would become obsolete'.[13] By the time Kant
was writing on religion, the liberal approach to the historicity of the
Scriptures was well under way. Indeed, Kant chided those whose
following of Jesus depended upon his metaphysical identity. We
should recognise the authority of the archetype regardless of the historicity or otherwise of the incarnation, miracles and life of Jesus.
Kant describes the person and work of Christ in terms devoid of reference to the supernatural. The central work of Christ lies in his
bringing a Kantian message of the freedom of the will to choose morally. Concerning the resurrection and ascension Kant has little pa-
tience. He describes these as later additions to the gospel accounts
valuable only as symbolic ways of describing the hope of eternal life.
Kant embarks on a process of interpreting miracles as symbols in a
way that prefigures Hick's interpretation of doctrines as mythological. The atonement is subjected to just such an interpretation. The
moral requirement of men and women to suffer and die to selfishness
each day 'is pictured as a death endured once for all by the representative of mankind'.[14] This analysis permits Kant to continue to use the
language of incarnation, atonement and resurrection but all reinterpreted as pictorial language, designed to convey truths otherwise
accessible through pure reason.

Though this treatment of miracles has a heavy influence on his
Christology, Kant cannot simply be described as anti-supernatural-
ist. While he does not deny that miracles may have occurred, he
does deny that miracles should be treated as foundations for religious belief. Miracles that really happened, like any historic events,
are never absolutely certain, nor absolutely necessary for belief. The
truth or falsity of the Christian religion stands or falls with the
self-authenticating status of its moral claims: 'If a moral religion
(which must consist not in dogmas and rites but in the heart's dispo-
sition to fulfil all human duties as divine commands) is to be
established, all *miracles* which history connects with its inauguration
must themselves in the end render superfluous the belief in miracles
in general'.[15]

---

[13] Allen, *The Human Christ*, 123.
[14] Kant, *Religion*, 69. See also 119–20.
[15] Kant, *Religion*, 79.

The validity of moral commands does not lie in the contingent events of history, but is already engraved on the human heart. Miracles are ultimately irrelevant to the moral essence of religion. This treatment of the essence of religion, sharing features with that of Hick, leads to a concept of religion as universal.

Universal Religion

Kant is committed to the idea that moral religion must have universal applicability. Every man and woman must be capable of following moral religion. Therefore, there is no significant religious knowledge that is tied to particular historical events, people or revelation – all that is necessary for true religion may be discerned through the exercise of pure reason. Joseph Runzo points out that the universal validity of religion is based upon Kant's assumption 'that any rational being who possesses the appropriate conceptual resources will arrive at the same, fully epistemically justified conclusions'.[16] The difference between moral (universal) religion and particular religions is that only pure moral religion 'can be believed in and shared by everyone', while 'an historical faith, grounded solely on facts, can extend its influence no further than tidings of it can reach'.[17] To restrict religion to its historical peculiarities, miracles, and so forth, is to confuse the core of religion with the external trappings in which it appears. The core of religion is moral transformation. The moral law necessary for this transformation is available through reason and does not require revelation.

It is worth making a note at this point of Kant's own terminology, which differs from contemporary usage. Kant describes as 'faiths' the particular religions of Judaism, Islam and Christianity along with the particular church groupings of Catholicism and Lutheranism. Underlying these faiths he identifies the '*one* (true) *religion*'.[18] So 'faiths' are particular examples of the universal religion. Wilfred Cantwell Smith uses the opposite terminology in his argument that faith is a general category present throughout the

---

[16] Runzo, *World-Views and Perceiving God*, 102.

[17] Kant, *Religion*, 94.

[18] Kant, *Religion*, 98.

world, whereas religions are historical manifestations of that faith.[19] Hick continues the more successful terminology of Smith but uses the same underlying distinction made by Kant. Hick identifies faith as the universal dimension of religious experience underlying the diverse, specific religions of the world.

For Kant, no one living in isolation from the specific traditions of Christianity is any worse off in relation to the divine being. The moral transformation that is the essence of faith is accessible to every person: 'they who seek to become well-pleasing to Him not by praising Him (or his envoy, as a being of divine origin) according to revealed concepts which not every man can have, but by a good course of life, regarding which everyone knows His will – these are they who offer Him the true veneration which He desires'.[20]

The concept of special revelation is, at best, redundant in Kant's theology. The value of particular faiths lies in the extent to which they encourage moral behaviour. He respects the Bible not because it is a revelation but because it seems to offer the best moral teachings. This positive assessment has to be seriously qualified by the fact that Kant has little interest in the real meaning of the Bible, only in the way it may be interpreted: 'an exposition of the revelation which has come into our possession is required, that is, a thoroughgoing interpretation of it in a sense agreeing with the universal practical rules of a religion of pure reason'.[21]

Kant even concedes that the interpretation may be 'forced' and may therefore completely depart from the literal interpretation of the text; but as long as one's interpretation of the text produces results in agreement with moral reason, it is valid. Kant offers his moral philosophy as a higher authority than the Bible. He points out that this process of interpretation has always been engaged in by Jews, Christians, Hindus and Muslims in order to reconcile some of the darker passages of their scriptures with the moral commands of pure reason.[22]

Doctrines, scriptures and historical events all serve a purpose in religious life in bringing men and women to an understanding of

---

[19] Smith, *The Meaning and End of Religion*, esp. 170–92.

[20] Kant, *Religion*, 95–6.

[21] Kant, *Religion*, 100.

[22] Kant, *Religion*, 102.

moral religion. However, when one grasps the moral demand of pure religion, then all such things may be dispensed with. Universal religion is compatible with any and every faith though it also supersedes or transcends them. We may establish this argument more clearly with reference to another feature of Kant's thought, a feature that became foundational for later twentieth-century religious studies.

The History of Religion

Kant's interpretation of Judaism is certainly faulty. Indeed, his account shares features with the general anti-Semitism of his time, which, within a century and a half, would lead to the most intense persecution of the Jews ever seen. But, leaving aside the question of the validity of his interpretation, we can identify a general Kantian approach to religion shared by Hick. It is an evolutionary approach to religion, drawing a distinction between primitive, this-worldly faith, and developed, transcendent faith. For Kant, Judaism is an example of the former: 'Judaism is really not a religion at all but merely a union of a number of people who, since they belonged to a particular stock, formed themselves into a commonwealth under purely political laws . . . it was *intended* to be merely an earthly state.'[23]

Kant dismisses Judaism for being merely a collection of political laws. As a faith it fails to direct anyone to transcendent significance and its concern with morality is directed only at outer observance, not inner change. He assumes, wildly inaccurately, that Judaism has never held to a belief in an afterlife and that this makes it impossible for Judaism to hold any notion of ultimate reward or blessing. Such an interpretation makes Judaism incompatible with Kant's view of real religion. A further feature of Judaism's incompatible with Kantian thought is the doctrine of election: that Israel was a nation chosen, or elected, by God. Kant merely repeated the anti-Semitism of his time by declaring that this doctrine expressed Jewish 'enmity toward all other peoples and which, therefore, evoked the enmity of all'.[24] Essentially, Judaism was an example of primitive

---

[23] Kant, *Religion*, 116.
[24] Kant, *Religion*, 117.

religion, only dimly expressing any sense of true moral religion. The function of such primitive religion was primarily one of maintaining socio-political order and stability among people in the face of chaos and disorder.

Addressing the development of religion after Judaism, Kant follows what we have already described as an evolutionary scheme. Evolutionary theory is far more widely applicable than merely to narrow biological concerns. Indeed, evolutionary approaches to religion have been deeply influential. Kant acknowledges that Christianity arose from Judaism, but affirms that it brought an entirely new principle of morality. Christianity, along with other major religions, is now in a process of continuing evolution as it faces the future. The particular world religions are really vehicles for the one, true, moral religion that will one day emerge. Kant believes that the prophets speak of a hope that eventually pure moral religion will entirely replace the mythological forms in which that religion is currently found. Following the evolutionary process, 'in the end religion will gradually be freed from all empirical determining grounds and from all statutes which rest on history'.[25] The myths of doctrine and supposed historical events all serve an interim purpose of helping men and women to realise a higher good in their lives. Yet such particularities are only of provisional use and, unless discarded, will obstruct the realisation of true universal religion.

This leads Kant to predict future history as marked by the gradual abandonment of historic faiths until 'at last the pure religion of reason will rule over all'.[26] This thought is best expressed in Kant's notion of an ethical commonwealth as the goal of human improvement. While it is true that people should act morally as an end in itself, without thought to the consequences, nonetheless the kingdom of virtue must be the necessary goal of moral endeavour. From the perspective of this ultimate end, empirical faiths are of somewhat mixed value. On the one hand, a religion may help point men and women to matters of higher value but, on the other hand, it obstructs that goal insofar as they promote their own dogmas and rites as of absolute value. It is only the moral element of the faiths that is to be praised and that will endure.

---

[25] Kant, *Religion*, 112.
[26] Kant, *Religion*, 112.

Hick's Debt to Kant

We may summarise Kant's treatment of religion in terms of the four themes already outlined:

1. His anthropology presupposes a form of libertarian free will and the inherent possibility of good behaviour in all people. The moral law is accessible to all people through the exercise of pure reason.
2. His treatment of the incarnation illustrates his general antipathy to historical particularities as being peripheral to the real purpose of religion.
3. The essence of religion as it is found universally is the concern with moral transformation.
4. Humanity's religious consciousness has been evolving away from primitive, nationalistic, this-worldly religion (Judaism) towards a higher religion concerned with the moral demands of pure reason.

Now we may review these four themes in relation to their treatment in the work of Hick.

Hick on freedom and morality

Hick's epistemology requires a libertarian view of free will. We have described his theory in terms of three steps from natural interpretation, through moral interpretation, to religious interpretation. The increasingly voluntary nature of each step arises from the ascending order of significance of each step. Hick describes the religious interpretation of the universe as a total interpretation because, while it involves its own distinctive religious experience, it also subsumes both moral and natural interpretation. Therefore, religion arises from moral and natural experience. This is similar to Kant's claim that morality precedes, and takes precedence over, religious beliefs. Hick is as convinced as Kant that one may successfully interpret the moral significance of the universe without taking the further step of interpreting the universe in the categories of a particular religious tradition. This picture of religious knowledge uncouples the connection between religion and morality. It is thus not surprising that Hick claims that the essence of morality is something we are all, theist or atheist, able to discern. Hick identifies the essence of morality as the demand to treat others as of the same value as oneself. This is a teaching embedded in Christ's teaching in the Sermon on the Mount, in various scriptures of the world religions, and 'is a translation of Kant's concepts of a rational person as an end, and of right action as action which our rationality, acknowledging a universal impartiality transcending individual desires and aversions, can see to be required'.[27]

Hick shares with Kant his confidence that morality is based upon universal truths anyone could arrive at through the exercise of pure reason. Furthermore, the pursuit of these moral demands does not require a special work of God's grace or revelation. As we saw with Kant, this does lead to a form of salvation by works. To be saved is identified with being committed to living life in a way that will be judged worthy. Hick joins Kant in what is in effect an endorsement of Pelagianism. Pelagius, like Hick and Kant, was a critic of Augustinian views of sin and salvation, and attacked Augustine's notion of original sin on the grounds that it compromised human free will: 'Everything good and everything evil, in respect of which we are either worthy of praise or of blame, is *done by us*, not *born with us*. We are not born in our full development, but with a capacity for good and evil'.[28]

Pelagius makes the same logical point that Kant would make centuries later: if one had no choice but to do evil, then one would not be responsible for it. Hick joins Pelagius and Kant in their commitment to libertarian free will. They all distinguish morality from religion, such that any human being both knows and is able to choose good, whether he or she has any knowledge of Christianity or not. At best, Kant's view of salvation implies a kind of partnership between God and people. As Michalson describes Kant's view of salvation, 'We have here something like a postulation of human/ divine cooperation in the recovery from radical evil, based on what amounts to a Pelagian appeal to divine assistance for those who do their moral best.'[29] However, given Kant's radical re-evaluation of

---

[27] Hick, *Interpretation*, 149.

[28] Pelagius, *Pro libero arbitrio* in Bettenson, *Documents of the Christian Church*, 53.

[29] Michalson, *Kant*, 115.

the doctrine of God, it is hard to see what real additional element such a being could bring. Indeed, Kant's religion of reason provides a basis for morality entirely independent of historic faiths, with their excess baggage of doctrine and ritual. Kant's vision of the future is that 'in the end religion will gradually be freed from all empirical determining grounds'.[30] Hick makes just the same distinction: 'In principle, then, and to a considerable extent in practice, we can separate out basic moral values from both the magical-scientific and the metaphysical beliefs which have always entered into their application within particular cultures.'[31]

Salvation is able to occur wherever there are human beings, because all are free and able to choose right moral values. Saving faith is thus identified with moral transformation.

Hick on the incarnation and other doctrinal claims

Hick and Kant share a programme of demythologising the language of religion into terms largely compatible with naturalism. They both regard the great, distinctive doctrines of Christianity as representational or symbolic uses of language. In his contribution to the *The Myth of God Incarnate* collection, Hick offered a demythologised account of the incarnation. As we have seen, this involved a rejection of the literal view as being logically incoherent. The real Jesus was simply a man with a powerful, indeed overwhelming, experience of divine reality. The metaphor Son of God or God the Son is a linguistic device which 'offers a way of declaring his significance to the world; and it expresses a disciple's commitment to Jesus as his personal Lord'.[32] The device was used by the early followers of Jesus as a poetic means of describing their commitment to what Jesus represented. Such poetry became crude, literalistic doctrine in the later church, and Hick offers his own work simply as an attempt to recover the real meaning of the language of incarnation.

In *The Metaphor of God Incarnate* the atonement is also subjected to this treatment and understood to be a pictorial use of language. Hick rejects the doctrine of original sin, for which atonement is

---

[30] Kant, *Religion*, 112.

[31] Hick, *An Interpretation of Religion*, 312.

[32] Hick, 'Jesus and the World Religions' in Hick (ed.), *The Myth of God Incarnate*, 178.

required, as a literal truth and interprets it 'as a mythological way of referring to the fact of universal human imperfection'.[33] He also rejects belief in a historic fall of humankind as totally unbelievable in the light of modern geology and anthropology. To retain the language of the fall is to use mythological language: 'we can say that the earliest humans were, metaphorically speaking, already "fallen" in the sense of being morally and spiritually imperfect'.[34] The metaphysical reality of atonement is also abandoned by Hick in favour of a mythological interpretation of this doctrine. Hick portrays much of church history as having been a struggle to get away from a literal view of the atonement, and in *The Rainbow of Faiths* suggests that a gathering consensus now interprets the doctrine as pictorial language:

> And so the death of Jesus has become for many Christians today the manifestation of a self-giving love which is an earthly reflection of the divine love, rather than an astonishing transaction to enable God to forgive sinners. But this represents a transformation of Christian understanding that would, until within about the last century, have seemed utterly heretical and, at one time, deserving the direst penalties.[35]

Hick's view of religious language as metaphor or myth causes him constantly to seek a literal core of meaning. To speak about atonement is simply to make use of a story that describes someone giving themselves, even to death, in their love for others. This seems a strange interpretation given the apparent futility of Christ's death. Jesus did not die fighting oppressors, sabotaging Roman instruments of war, or leading a protest in the streets – he died on a technical charge of blasphemy, abandoned by his followers, without offering any inspiring, Socrates-like speech. In what sense Jesus gave himself for others when he died, if not as a literal atonement, Hick does not say. In this way the history of the death of Jesus is distinguished from the stories we tell about it. It is those stories with which we are concerned, in Hick's view of doctrine, not the real

---

[33] Hick, *The Metaphor of God Incarnate*, 115.
[34] Hick, *Metaphor*, 116.
[35] Hick, *The Rainbow of Faiths*, 130–1.

historical events. However, he provides no analysis of what historic basis underlies those stories and why they should matter so much to us today.

A clear pattern emerges in Hick's treatment of the incarnation and atonement, which, if taken literally, would cause one to stumble into too many logical and historical problems. When one encounters such logical difficulties the language should be interpreted as myth or metaphor, not as literal. This process allows any religious claims to be harmonised with the pluralist hypothesis.

Kant pursues a similar hermeneutic. He distinguishes between knowledge gained from history and knowledge universally accessible through reason. Particular, historical knowledge is not universally accessible and, consequently for Kant, cannot be universally necessary: 'We have noted that a Church dispenses with the most important mark of truth, namely, a rightful claim to universality, when it bases itself upon a revealed faith. For such a faith, being historical . . . can never be universally communicated so as to produce conviction.'[36]

For this reason Kant also embarks on a reductive analysis of key Christian beliefs so that those beliefs related to specific historical events can be shed in favour of their supposed universal meaning. We have noted that Kant describes Christ as the archetype of moral perfection. As an archetype Jesus represents a moral quality to which every man and woman already has access. The doctrine of Christ is a helpful exposition of this truth, but it is not necessary. People may grasp the truth without knowing or assenting to the literal teachings. Furthermore, the doctrines of the atonement or the Trinity are also subjected to this analysis. The value of such doctrines lies not in their correspondence to literal reality, but in the way they encourage moral improvement. Hick describes the doctrine of the Trinity not as a literal revelation of the nature of God, but as informing us that there are at least 'three ways in which the one God is humanly thought and experienced'.[37] Taken this way, the Trinity is an illustration of the pluralist hypothesis: God is experienced and described in a plurality of forms. Kant describes the doctrine as informing us that 'God wills to be served under three

---

[36] Kant, *Religion*, 100.
[37] Hick, *Metaphor*, 149.

specifically different moral aspects.'[38] This suggests that the doctrine is better taken as a presupposition of moral behaviour. Hick finds in the doctrine of the Trinity an underlying statement of the pluralist hypothesis. Kant finds in the doctrine a pictorial statement of his own ethical proposals. Both thinkers find in this profound doctrine a symbolic description of their own philosophical proposals.

Kant and Hick describe Christian doctrine as largely incoherent by the standards of reason. As metaphors doctrines remain helpful in encouraging moral behaviour; but if one wants to understand the real meaning of religion, then one must strip away such verbal embellishments and discover the underlying, universal truth. This process rests on a certain view of metaphorical language, which we shall have reason to question in Chapter 8.

Hick on the nature of universal religion

In order to sustain his notion of the universal accessibility of salvation Kant maintains that the core of religion lies in essential moral rules. He distinguishes between moral religion and historic faiths: '*Pure religious faith* alone can found a universal church; for only (such) rational faith can be believed in and shared by everyone'.[39] Historical faiths dependent upon particular revelation or unique events have not been and cannot be shared by everyone, so they do not represent the core of religion. Hick pursues a similar line of thought and also distinguishes between the essence of religion and its particular forms. An example of this is found in his treatment of conflicting truth claims. While they might, in principle, be settled by historical research, on the whole they concern matters not readily accessible to scholarship. In any case, Hick suggests that a growing number of people, himself included, 'no longer regard such questions as being of the essence of their faith'.[40] If one does not join this groundswell of opinion and prefers to maintain that some historical event, such as the incarnation, is in some way essential to faith, then, Hick concedes, the pluralist project would hold no appeal: 'But it remains true that for many other believers [historical

---

[38] Kant, *Religion*, 132.

[39] Kant, *Religion*, 94.

[40] Hick, *Interpretation*, 365.

claims] *are* of the essence of their faith, so that no amount of evidence could ever change their conviction, and that for such persons the pluralist vision may well at present be inaccessible.'[41]

Such attachment to historical events is to be found in all the great religions and so the pluralist account will find its critics in every quarter. Nonetheless, within all religions one does find similar moral commands. In particular, the golden rule of Christ is to be found in various forms throughout the world religions. Given that Hick and Kant share a soteriology that bears all the hallmarks of Pelagianism it is not surprising that these moral principles are seen as the essence of religion. Matters of dispute are, at best, secondary issues. By reframing many of these secondary matters as mythological Hick is able to harmonise them with his proposed essence of religion.

Hick on the history of religions

There is a certain parallel to the treatments of religious history found in Hick and Kant. Hick treats the history of religions in terms of two stages, the first being the *pre-axial* stage of religion. These are the very ancient, often pre-literate, religions that still exist today in some parts of the world. Pre-axial religions are excluded from Hick's pluralist account as they do not share the broader vision of the great world religions that arose after the flowering of religious consciousness in the *axial* age. There are two dimensions to pre-axial religions. Firstly, they have a *psychological* function in helping people make some sense of life and death. Secondly, they have a *sociological* function, which Hick describes as 'preserving the unity of the tribe or people within a common world-view and at the same time of validating the community's claims upon the loyalty of its members'.[42] They are not concerned with grand metaphysical doctrines of life after death or of a transcendent being. Life beyond the grave, though throughout history assumed to be a real prospect, was described in dark, shadowy terms. It was an existence more to be feared than envied.

---

[41] Hick, *Interpretation*, 365.
[42] Hick, *Interpretation*, 23.

Kant describes Judaism in remarkably similar terms to Hick's treatment of pre-axial religion. Hick would place Judaism in the later axial period; but if one simply replaces Judaism with pre-axial religions, then Kant's view is not so far different. We have already seen that Kant denies that Judaism is really a religion at all. Early, or pure, Judaism was merely a political organisation. It was concerned merely with outward appearances, social cohesion and tribal security. It guarded racial purity against the forces of chaos. According to Kant, Judaism did not offer worship to a transcendent, moral being. The Jewish God is 'merely an earthly regent making absolutely no claims upon, and no appeals to, conscience'.[43] Kant also denies that Judaism has any significant concept of life after death. Hick would disown the accuracy of Kant's treatment of Judaism, but happily applies similar terms to pre-axial religion.

We have seen an evolutionary scheme underlying Kant's notion of religious development. Hick describes this kind of development in terms of the axial age (approximately 800–200 BC), borrowing this framework from the writings of Karl Jaspers.[44] This is the second stage in his history of religion. It gave rise to a new era of cosmic optimism in religion. Hick notes that during this period all the major religious options were formed, and each shares a common assumption that moral transformation of the individual is both desirable and possible: 'Thus all these post-axial faiths are soteriologically oriented.'[45] The common essence of post-axial faiths is the golden rule of moral duty to one's neighbour as if acting towards oneself. According to Kant, Christianity marks a complete break with Judaism at this point. Its defining feature is that it 'was to comprise a religion valid for the world'[46] and not just a tribal or local political grouping. Christianity is, then, a supreme statement of the moral religion of pure reason; but this universal religion is still present, in other forms, in all the historic faiths. Hick does not grant any supremacy to Christianity, but he does identify a core of teaching that is

---

[43] Kant, *Religion*, 116.
[44] Jaspers, *The Origin and Goal of History*, esp. 51–60.
[45] Hick, *Interpretation*, 33.
[46] Kant, *Religion*, 118.

post-axial and present in all the major world religions.[47] Kant shares this conviction that moral religion is universally available to the higher state of religious awareness: 'The one true religion comprises nothing but laws, that is, those practical principles of whose unconditioned necessity we can become aware, and which we therefore recognise as revealed through pure reason (not empirically).'[48]

Matters of history, dogma and ritual may constitute the concrete form of a religion, but for both Hick and Kant moral duty lies at its heart. The increasing extent to which this is recognised, and other matters seen as mythological, is part of the increasing evolution of religion towards its purer state.

Conclusion

We clearly see many similarities between Kant and Hick's treatment of religion, going far beyond Hick's acknowledged debt to a Kantian epistemology. One may simplify Kant's positive theological position as an affirmation of two basic postulates: the existence of God and a continued personal existence beyond physical death in which one will gain the ultimate reward for right behaviour. The difference between the two thinkers is that for Hick these are postulates of religious experience rather than being postulates of practical (moral) reason. However, even this difference is muted when one acknowledges that for Hick religious experience is simply a more profound form of moral experience. It is the third step of interpretation that goes beyond, but also depends upon, the second step of moral knowledge.

Is Hick conscious of the extent of his dependence upon Kant? Probably not. Hick makes little reference to Kant's wider work in his own writings. While many commentators describe Hick as Kantian, few would want to press the connection as far as I have done here. For example, Paul Eddy describes Hick's mature work as

---

[47] Of course, Christianity, along with Islam and Sikhism, arose chronologically after the axial age, but Hick identifies these traditions as simply a continuation of the discoveries made in that period.

[48] Kant, *Religion*, 156.

a neo-Kantian proposal but adds the following qualification: 'The term "neo-Kantian" is used throughout this essay in a very general sense; it implies no connection to the German philosophical movement of the late nineteenth and early twentieth centuries.'[49] However, we can identify a stronger connection than this. Hick is thoroughly Kantian in his commitments. How then can we explain the lack of specific references? The answer lies in the fact that Hick belongs to a more general movement of which Kant was, in many ways, the founding figure. They both share a commitment to the common Enlightenment project. Hick arrives at similar conclusions to Kant because he belongs to a tradition based upon a shared epistemology. Regardless of the extent to which Hick acknowledges this or gives specific reference to Kant, the fact is that he is driven to the pluralist hypothesis because its seeds were already planted in early Enlightenment thought. We now turn to identify this major cultural movement of which Kant and Hick could be seen, in a sense, to be the bookends; one standing at its introduction and the other at its conclusion.

---

[49] Eddy, 'Religious Pluralism and the Divine: Another look at John Hick's Neo-Kantian Proposal', 467. See also D'Costa, 'John Hick and Religious Pluralism: Yet Another Revolution', 4; Loughlin, 'Noumenon and Phenomena', 497–8; Ramachandra, *The Recovery of Mission*, 117–25.

Chapter 7

Pluralism and the Enlightenment

In previous chapters we have traced two sources for Hick's thought.
The first was the tradition of scepticism, and the second the philosophy of Kant. These two traditions intertwine as Kant sought to
resolve the challenge of scepticism. We did not conclude, however,
that Hick is consciously appropriating the entire theological project
of Kant, for there are many differences between these thinkers.
Nonetheless, we noted many striking similarities in their work and
it takes little imagination to see that Kant's theology would lead naturally to Hick's ethical pluralism. The reason why their thought is
so similar is that they are both part of the major cultural movement
of the west known as modernism or Enlightenment thought. In this
chapter I shall set out this wider context in which to place Hick's
theological proposal. What we shall then find is that religious pluralism is a natural consequence of Enlightenment philosophy.

The Break with Tradition

Kant described the cultural and philosophical changes of his own
times, while also being key in bringing those changes about. He saw
his age as making a radical break with the past. Most commentators
date the movement known as modernism from the work of
Descartes;[1] in particular his philosophy which turned attention from
the authority of traditions to the authority of the thinking self. This

---

[1] E.g. Allen, *Christian Belief in a Postmodern World*, 37; Küng, *Does God
Exist?*, 5ff.; Middleton and Walsh, *Truth Is Stranger than it Used to Be*, 41;
Newbigin, *The Gospel in a Pluralist Society*, 28.

heralded the key theme of the Enlightenment. In this way, the seeds of modernism were sown. However, Descartes's own work remained part of the late mediaeval worldview rather than truly breaking with the past. After all, his method still relied heavily on a proof for the existence of God as a foundation for philosophy; thus methodologically distancing him from key characteristics of later modernism.[2] Kant does make a decisive break with the past, though, and he demands that others join him in this radical break:

> Enlightenment is man's release from his self-incurred tutelage. Tutelage is man's inability to make use of his understanding without direction from another. Self-incurred is this tutelage when its cause lies not in lack of reason but in lack of resolution and courage to use it without direction from another. *Sapere aude!* 'Have courage to use your own reason' – that is the motto of enlightenment.[3]

In this call to enlightenment Kant makes clear two key features that will mark the movement. Firstly, it is a complete break with the past. By 'tutelage' Kant means any institution that imposes truth, meaning or morality from above: tutelage is an imposition from a higher authority. While it could be despotic in form, this need not be the case. Indeed, Kant saw its basic form, as the eighteenth century drew to a close in Prussia, as something 'self-incurred' because the people were lazy – they wanted it that way. Just as a child spoilt by its parents grows lazy, so the population had come to enjoy not having to think for themselves. Enlightenment would be the intellectual act of breaking rank with such imposed authority. It was to be humanity's coming of age. Whether Protestant or Catholic in form, the traditions of Christianity were clear examples of the shackles from which Kant urged people to break free.

The second key feature is summed up in the call '*Sapere aude!*' (Dare to know!). The way to knowledge and understanding is not through blind obedience to a tradition, but through the autonomous use of reason. Kant describes this summons as a call to 'go alone' in contrast to the slavish obedience of the masses, which he

---

[2] Gellner shows the significance of this in *Reason and Culture*, 1–22.
[3] Kant, *On History*, 3.

compares to 'domestic cattle' – dumb, placid and conformist.[4] The person who truly enters the Enlightenment leaves behind the mass of humanity, herded along in their communities, believing only what they are told. This independent, uncoerced exercise of human reason is the other vital feature of enlightenment.

The most obvious traditions with which Kant took issue were religious traditions. There are also traditions of art, philosophy and science, but Kant does not perceive these to be such a threat to enlightenment: 'I have placed the main point of enlightenment . . . chiefly in matters of religion because our rulers have no interest in playing the guardian with respect to the arts and sciences and also because religious incompetence is not only the most harmful but also the most degrading of all.'[5]

Religion seemed to have special protection in the post-Reformation world, a protection not extended to art or science. These latter disciplines were the subjects of free public debate and open to revision and reformulation wherever necessary. In contrast, religion was not being subjected to this kind of revision: it exercised an authority that held itself to be beyond criticism. At least this is how it felt to Kant in eighteenth-century Prussia. The Reformation clearly subjected religious authorities to debate and analysis, but, through the passage of time, religious traditions had stabilised and new forms of authoritarianism were in place. Today, with the passing of time, one notices that the arts and the sciences are not as freely open to public debate as one might wish. The sciences, in particular, are capable of taking on an authoritarian status that tolerates no dissent.[6] This is an important theme to which we shall return when we consider modernism itself as a religion.

Kant heralded, perhaps even set in motion, a shift in western culture as significant as the Reformation. The age of enlightenment had begun and with it a reappraisal of religious traditions. One particular forum for this reappraisal would be the Gifford Lectures. Lord Adam Gifford (1820–87) left in his will instructions and

---

[4] Kant, *History*, 3.
[5] Kant, *History*, 9.
[6] Kuhn gives evidence for this in *The Structure of Scientific Revolutions*, 144–59.

finances to support a series of lectures in natural theology at the Scottish universities. His will specified that the lectures would treat religion 'as a strictly natural science' in which it would be 'considered just as astronomy or chemistry is'.[7] As a matter of fact, natural theology was losing its influence by the time the lectures were instituted and that explains the diversity of theologians who would give them. Lecturers would include Karl Barth, Emil Brunner, Rudolph Bultmann, J.G. Frazer, William James, Michael Polanyi, Paul Tillich and A.N. Whitehead.[8] Nonetheless, the original purpose of the endowment reflects the attitude of the Enlightenment towards religion. Alasdair MacIntyre, another Gifford lecturer and a critic of natural theology, describes the worldview of Gifford and his contemporaries as dominated by the 'guiding presupposition of thought that substantive rationality is unitary, that there is a single, if perhaps complex, conception of what the standards and achievements of rationality are, one by which every educated person can without too much difficulty be brought to agree in acknowledging'.[9]

The age of enlightenment brought a great optimism regarding the use of reason. Just as such progress was being made in astronomy and chemistry, why should there not be dramatic progress in our understanding of religion and morality? The intention of the Gifford Lectures was to establish a firm, rational footing from which all the varied religious traditions of the world could be surveyed and assessed. Natural theology was prized, while revealed theology was dismissed. Hick's *An Interpretation of Religion* was originally given as the Gifford Lectures of 1986–87. Regarding their published form, Paul Badham comments, 'Lord Gifford would have been delighted by this book. It is hard to think of any previous Gifford Lectures which more precisely fulfilled the terms of the will.'[10] Gifford had belonged to the movement of modernism with its commitment to treating

---

[7] MacIntyre, *Three Rival Versions of Moral Enquiry*, 9.

[8] Wright, 'Gifford Lectures' in Ferguson and Wright (eds.), *New Dictionary of Theology*, 268–9.

[9] MacIntyre, *Versions*, 14.

[10] Badham, 'John Hick's *An Interpretation of Religion*' in Hewitt (ed.), *Problems in the Philosophy of Religion*, 86.

religion according to the scientific principles of the Enlightenment. Human reason and the principles of empirical enquiry
were to settle all differences and guide all enquiries, and Hick's
methodology fits well with this vision of enquiry.

Objectivity and Neutrality

MacIntyre notes this presupposition informing both the method
and aims of those involved in producing the ninth edition of the
Encyclopaedia Britannica. Given belief in a basic standard of rationality, the editors were optimistic that information from religion,
politics, morals, the arts and the sciences could be described in
purely objective terms. Bias, commitments, preferences and values
could be set to one side in the aim of producing an objective catalogue of knowledge. The ideal of the encyclopaedists was to present
objective 'knowledge rather than opinion'[11] and their hope was that
in the wake of the Enlightenment the 'Encyclopaedia would have
displaced the Bible as the canonical book . . . of the culture.'[12]

This drive towards a comprehensive, unifying conception of
knowledge was undertaken in terms quite different from those of
the mediaeval scholastics or the English Puritans. This was not a
religious, doctrinally oriented approach to unifying knowledge;
rather, it was based upon a commitment to the neutrality of
research. Philosophers of the Enlightenment, of which Kant is our
great example, argued for a method that would purge reason of its
biases and prejudices. In his groundbreaking treatment of the
Enlightenment, *Whose Justice? Which Rationality?*, MacIntyre
describes their proposal: 'It was a central aspiration of the Enlightenment, an aspiration the formulation of which was itself a great
achievement, to provide for debate in the public realm standards
and methods of rational justification by which alternative courses of
action in every sphere of life could be adjudged just or unjust, rational or irrational, enlightened or unenlightened.'[13]

---

[11] *Encyclopaedia Britannica* 1, viii (ninth edn., 1873). Cited in MacIntyre,
Versions, 19.
[12] MacIntyre, *Versions*, 19.
[13] MacIntyre, *Whose Justice? Which Rationality?*, 6.

These proposed standards would provide the neutral, universal vantage point from which all religious, moral and scientific claims could be adjudicated. The use of the judicial metaphor here is helpful as it draws attention to the great value invested in the principle of rationality. Human reason would be handed the reigns of power as arbitrating judge in place of the tutelage of tradition. Armed only with the resources of reason, Enlightenment thinkers sought to distinguish between cultural superstitions and the underlying truths of religion.

The high value of impartiality and neutrality has continued to be sought in the field of religious studies. The attraction of impartial, neutral reason is that it provides an acultural court of appeal to which all of humanity has access. Parochial claims to authority may have had their place in the Greek or European city-states, but in the light of global pluralism, with its diverse seats of authority, the liberalism of the Enlightenment offers great advantages. The neutral stance of modernist thought provides two significant tools for understanding religion.

The first of these is the possibility of a *universal language* in which truth can be expressed and tested. MacIntyre describes the cosmopolitan mentality of the Enlightenment as offering 'the confident belief that all cultural phenomena must be translucent to understanding, that all texts must be capable of being translated into the language which the adherents of modernity speak to each other'.[14] Such a universal language makes possible a common understanding of concepts, values and beliefs. It is the cultural equivalent to the symbolic language of mathematics, enabling its practitioners to transcend cultural particularities and enter the thought worlds of other people. It is hard to realise in our world of global communications just how radical this concept was at a time when all knowledge could be expressed in a single linguistic system. As far as religion was concerned, it would offer the possibility of a kind of theological Esperanto for the dissemination and interaction of thought.

The second tool provided by modernist claims to neutrality is a *universal form of reason*. The assumption that beliefs could be expressed in a common framework also implied that a common,

[14] MacIntyre, *Justice*, 327.

universal logic could be used to weigh and test those beliefs. In both rationality and morality, modernism presupposed an agreed standard of truth implicit in all cultures. In many cases it may be somewhat hidden, but Kant's epistemology made it clear that there are certain universal features of pure reason common to all humanity. Exceptions to this common standard of reason must be explained by an unsound mind, just as exceptions to a common standard of morality might be accounted for by some kind of mental illness. Modernism heralded a great optimism for the future of humankind, and intellectual emancipation was supposed to lead to such a consensus on moral and rational matters. All that stood in the way of this progress were ignorance and superstition. However, through the two world wars of the twentieth century this optimism was fatally wounded and a postmodern reaction arose. Nonetheless, the vestiges of modernism remain, and Hick's account of religious pluralism is just such an example.[15]

MacIntyre provides a helpful analysis and critique of modernism in terms of his concept of a tradition of enquiry. In Kant's great call to 'Dare to Know!' he urged the breaking of the shackles of tradition. However, as MacIntyre ruefully notes, Kant's own legacy was not the abandonment of tradition but the establishment of an alternative tradition. This tradition had to cope with one obvious failing of modernism: despite the optimism of the encyclopaedists, a consensus on rational and moral principles failed to emerge. Yet what might have been considered a flaw in modernism was turned into a cardinal virtue. Modernism led to liberalism in which the individual is encouraged to choose freely and live by

---

[15] Some critics identify Hick as a postmodernist (e.g. Cook, 'Postmodernism, Pluralism and John Hick', 10–11), and Hick has responded to this charge with some surprise (Hick, 'Reader's Responses', 20–21) given his own commitment to foundationalism. This leads Carson to comment on the exchange that there are two types of pluralist – those who own a position and those who disown any final theological position (Carson, *The Gagging of God*, 147). It might be concluded from such an exchange that postmodernism and modernism are much closer than their proponents would suggest. Even the most radical postmodern thought is the logical legacy of modernism. Suffice to say, this author wishes to be categorised as neither!

'whatever conception of the good he or she pleases'.[16] Liberalism claims to value social pluralism, a condition which must be affirmed in keeping with the golden rule of tolerance. Individuals are entitled to choose their own conception of the good – as long as holding to it will not prevent others from holding to their own conceptions of the good. In this way, liberalism holds its own absolute (i.e. tolerance) alongside its relativism.

The encyclopaedist vision, as MacIntyre describes it, may be summarised in the following way. It is the project stemming from the Enlightenment and continuing to the present day, which attempts to replace religious, civil or sovereign authority with the authority of human reason. It presupposes a common rationality and morality (at least the moral claim of tolerance) in which disputes may be settled. This vision, proposed by Kant and revised over two hundred years, has led to various forms of atheism (such as Marxism) and to Hick's pluralism. As we shall see, ultimately there is not much distance between these two resulting positions, as the movement of modernism, which is an umbrella term for this stream of thought, is itself a tradition to which they belong.

The Recovery of Tradition

MacIntyre uses the term 'tradition' to identify movements of intellectual enquiry that have given rise to their own public institutions and moral life.[17] A tradition is a homogenous community in which human thought and speculation are pursued. These may involve political structures, religious institutions, social arrangements, and concepts of justice. He demonstrates that only in the context of such traditions can intellectual enquiry occur. Traditions are not optional patterns of belief for those who can't go it alone. Indeed, there is no such 'going it alone' outside a tradition of enquiry: 'There is no standing ground, no place for enquiry, no way to

---

[16] MacIntyre, *Justice*, 336.
[17] There are a number of useful discussions of MacIntyre's account in Horton and Mendus (eds.), *After MacIntyre*. See also McMylor, *Alasdair MacIntyre: Critic of Modernity*, 147–73.

engage in the practices of advancing, evaluating, accepting, and rejecting reasoned argument apart from that which is provided by some particular tradition or other.'[18]

Traditions are the necessary standpoints from which moral and rational enquiry can be conducted. Traditions provide principles of reason, examples of morality, and precedents for new ideas. For this reason, MacIntyre considers the attempt to identify universal categories of reason or morality to be doomed. What then of Kant's claim to be throwing off the chains of tutelage? It can only mean that Kant was substituting one tradition for another; the tradition of Enlightenment reason for the tradition of orthodox Christianity.

If MacIntyre is correct then the encyclopaedists were mistaken to think that a common system of reason and language could systematise all knowledge. They may have thought they were doing this but, in effect, they were simply promoting their own tradition of enquiry above all others. MacIntyre writes in striking terms that, given a diversity of traditions with no possibility of taking the view from nowhere, 'there are, so it will turn out, rationalities rather than rationality, just as it will turn out that there are justices rather than justice'.[19] In one sense MacIntyre sounds like a relativist, but he is not. He is arguing, contra modernism, that we must recognise genuine pluralism in matters of reason and morality, but not concede that truth itself is plural. A Christian would claim to have discovered a truth that, at least, entails that some of the beliefs of non-Christians are false. However, there is no straightforward way of demonstrating why the non-Christian is mistaken – there is no neutral set of rational or moral rules that can arbitrate between Christian and non-Christian. To admit to belonging to a tradition of enquiry entails a certain methodological humility, but not relativism. The discipline of apologetics may seem much more difficult, but it is not impossible.

Some critics of the concept of a tradition of enquiry point out that it fails to take into account the fluidity of human thought. The work of Wilfred Cantwell Smith, in particular, has destroyed any simple notion of religions living in absolute isolation from one another: ideas cross-fertilise among the religious traditions of the

---

[18] MacIntyre, *Justice*, 350.
[19] MacIntyre, *Justice*, 9.

world. Traditions also develop and change. Furthermore, the possibility of conversion seems to suggest that one can decide, on certain grounds, to leave a tradition behind entirely and belong to a new one. Keith Ward points out that commitment to a tradition is much more than commitment to a rational system: 'Especially in the case of religious institutions, the reality of social membership is so complex and the reasons for membership so diverse that it would be quite false to think it was a matter of intellectual assent to all the declarations of the institution.'[20]

This point applies directly to why individuals may choose to belong or not belong to a tradition. Many social factors are involved in such decisions; it is not simply a matter of rational choice. However, MacIntyre's concept is less to do with individual choice and more to do with the status of a tradition as a whole. Whatever the reasons for individuals belonging there, the tradition as a whole does include its own principles of reason and morality. MacIntyre concedes that there are changes and developments, but points out that a core of constitutive belief remains the common thread that gives a tradition its historical coherence. If allegiance to those core beliefs is lost, then the tradition has died. There is some point at which development is so radical that the old is gone and something new has taken its place. When this occurs in the life of an individual, conversion has occurred. At the level of a community conversion might also occur.[21]

Modernism as a Religion

MacIntyre's description of tradition provides a helpful framework for understanding the varied streams of intellectual thought that come to dominate cultures. In particular, it emphasises that even the liberal-modernist movement is itself a tradition. It has no right to claim neutrality in its assessment of religious traditions, but is itself a tradition of enquiry with its own standards of reason and morality.

---

[20] Ward, *Religion and Revelation*, 43–4.
[21] This is parallel to Thomas Kuhn's description of the revolution that takes place in a scientific community through a paradigm shift. See Kuhn, *Structure*.

The work of the encyclopaedists represents one way in which the Enlightenment developed; and we find a theological example of the immediate impact of the Enlightenment in the thought of Friedrich Schleiermacher.

While Kant is a founding figure for the philosophy of modernism, Schleiermacher is a founding figure for its theology. With deep roots in Christian pietism, not unlike Kant, he sought to establish a basis for Christianity in the wake of the scepticism and growing secularism of his age. Schleiermacher was in many ways an apologist for Christianity as well as an innovator in theology. His twist on Kantian theology laid the ground for modern liberalism in its approach to the doctrines of God, humanity and Christ as well as promoting the new higher criticism of the Bible. As we found with Kant, so now with Schleiermacher we can identify many parallels with Hick's pluralist proposal. Indeed, as regards the relationship between faith and religious experience, Hick's proposal is very close to the work of Schleiermacher. This is no surprise, as there is an essential continuity running through the movement of modernism binding Kant, Schleiermacher and Hick together.[22]

While the Enlightenment period was not devoid of religious commitment, the kind of religion that came to dominate intellectual circles was not the Christianity of the eighteenth-century evangelical revival, but deism and rationalism. Kant himself, in many ways retaining his pietistic roots, produced a form of religion strong on moralism but weak on any experiential knowledge of God. Schleiermacher responded to the rationalism of the age with an account that identified the essence of Christianity in *Gerfühl* (feeling). The German word 'does not connote a sensation, as its English rendering would suggest, but a deep sense or awareness'.[23] Schleiermacher tried to show that it was a mistake to equate religion with ethics, as Kant had done, and miss this crucial dimension of religious feeling or awareness.

Schleiermacher notes that all our experience of other people is marked by the experience of 'dependence', a general quality of human feeling. However, there is also a higher stage of such experience: the feeling of absolute dependence. He writes that 'this feeling

---

[22] D'Costa, *John Hick's Theology of Religions*, 9.
[23] Grenz and Olson, *20th Century Theology*, 44.

of absolute dependence' is 'not an accidental element, or [*sic*] a thing which varies from person to person, but is a universal element of life; and the recognition of this fact entirely takes the place, for the system of doctrine, of all the so-called proofs of the existence of God'.[24]

Like Kant's categories, the feeling of absolute dependence is universal and self-evident. We cannot get behind the experience to test it; nor is it an additional component of knowledge that we must find or learn. This concept of feeling undercuts the uniqueness of Christianity. Rudolf Otto would later follow a similar path in using religious experience as the key theme in his interpretation of global religion.[25]

Although Christology remained important for Schleiermacher, he subjected it to a significant revision. He understood the significance of Jesus to be the degree to which the feeling of absolute dependence was realised in his person. Jesus had the highest form of that experience. Therefore, the difference between Jesus and the rest of humanity was more a matter of degree than kind. We find in him a more profound sense of a basic feeling we all share. This approach to the essence of Christianity clearly removes from it any unique or normative status in favour of something that is universal.

Kant and Schleiermacher both abandoned a doctrine of historic or special revelation in their respective revisions of theology. One can see how the concept of a tradition of authority easily arises from belief in special revelation; one must concede to the authority of specific, historical events, individuals and councils if one believes in a doctrine of special revelation. Throwing off the shackles of tradition required that the modernists locate authority elsewhere. Indeed, authority must be internalised if the self is to be guaranteed the autonomy that the Enlightenment urged us to find. Kant and Schleiermacher both heralded a Copernican revolution in their turn from external authority to subjective forms of authority. For Kant this ultimately led to moral thought, while for Schleiermacher it led to religious experience.

---

[24] Schleiermacher, *The Christian Faith*, 133–4.
[25] Otto, *The Idea of the Holy*.

An Analysis of Liberalism

George Lindbeck, who provides a helpful analysis of various theological movements in the western world, argues that liberalism
finds its roots in the work of Schleiermacher. Lindbeck describes
liberalism as an experiential-expressivist approach to doctrine. An
assumption of this movement is that 'the scholarly study of religious
phenomena on the whole supports the crucial affirmations of the
basic unity of religious experience'.[26] Religious experience is held
to be the key to interpreting the wide variety of beliefs and practices
both within the church and in relation to religious pluralism. The
need for such a key came in the wake of Kant's devastating analysis
of religion. Lindbeck describes the achievement of Kant as the
'reduction of God to a transcendental condition of morality'.[27]
Schleiermacher's response to this reductionism was a theory of
religion with experience as its core: in contrast to orthodoxy, doctrines were no longer to be assessed as realist claims regarding a
cognitive reality, but as expressions of felt experience. In a sense,
Schleiermacher is just as committed to reductionism as Kant,
though the commitment leads his thought elsewhere.

Schleiermacher is a classic example of the experiential-
expressivist approach to religion. In the twentieth century one
might have supposed that this would make Karl Rahner its major
exponent, as this Roman Catholic theologian owes much to the
anthropology of Schleiermacher. Although Rahner proposes an
inclusivist approach to religions rather than a pluralist account,
Lindbeck describes him as a hybrid thinker who does not neatly fit
the expressivist stream of thought. John Hick is a much more
straightforward example of an expressivist. He is a qualified
expressivist in that he accepts the realist cognitive account of religion, positing an objective reality as the object of religious devotion.
However, he considers our only contact with that presupposed
objective reality is mediated through an indirect, subjective experience. Therefore, whatever qualification Hick's wider work might
suggest to this description, he can certainly be described as a *practical*
expressivist. Though there is a formal commitment to a divine

---

[26] Lindbeck, *The Nature of Doctrine*, 32.
[27] Lindbeck, *Doctrine*, 21.

reality 'out there', the true concern of religion is with a feeling in our own hearts. Though Rahner and Hick develop their own thought in radically different directions they both share a common heritage in the Enlightenment project. This may be shown more clearly as we briefly review Lindbeck's analysis of expressivism.

The success of the experiential-expressivist approach to religious doctrine is explained by its ability to deal with social and religious pluralism. Doctrines that would otherwise be divisive may be resolved or at least marginalised in the expressivist framework. Where the cognitive approach to doctrine had emphasised the literal meaning of doctrinal claims, the expressivist emphasises an underlying non-verbal religious experience. This experience had given rise to those claims and takes precedence over them, and may be universal, though expressed in different doctrinal forms among different cultures. Theologies of religious pluralism follow naturally from this framework: 'The rationale suggested, though not necessitated, by an experiential-expressive approach is that the various religions are diverse symbolisations of one and the same core experience of the Ultimate, and that therefore they must respect each other, learn from each other, and reciprocally enrich each other.'[28]

The cognitive approach leads to 'exclusivism' with its separation among religious traditions over their confessions and creeds. In contrast, the expressivist approach leads to theological pluralism. Religious creeds are granted only a relative status as symbolic ways of explaining a more basic experience. Expressivism is the basic framework of liberalism and the modernist movement of which Hick is a contemporary example. While early forms of expressivism, such as that found in Schleiermacher and continued in Rahner, seek to maintain the superiority of Christianity over non-Christian religion, this attempt is doomed. Expressivism leads inexorably to some form of philosophical pluralism: 'When religions are thought of as expressively rather than propositionally true, this possibility of complementarity and mutual enrichment is increased, but it also becomes hard to attach any definite meaning to the notion of "unsurpassably true".'[29]

---

[28] Lindbeck, *Doctrine*, 23.

[29] Lindbeck, *Doctrine*, 49.

The world religions are taken to be different symbolic expressions of the same underlying experience. Therefore, the knowledge of God varies among religions by a matter of *degree* not as a matter of *kind*. One religion may have a greater degree of religious knowledge than others, but it is impossible to describe a religion as having knowledge of a different kind. Thus all that Schleiermacher and Rahner can claim is that Christianity has a higher intensity or better expression of that experience. But such claims can only be provisional. Knowledge being a matter of degree, not kind, there is no quality that prevents someone else or another religion developing a better expression of that experience. For an expressivist to claim that Christianity is 'unsurpassably' true just looks like prejudice. There is no theoretical reason why the experience of a Christian or the creeds of Christianity might not be surpassed by others.

The drawbacks and difficulties of expressivism reflect the problems bound up in the Kantian attempt to step outside any tradition. One logical problem with this method of arriving at a pluralist theology is that it sets out to prove a conclusion that is already assumed in its methodology: expressivist theologians seek to identify a common experience underlying varied religious traditions. Despite all the doctrinal variations among religions, expressivists believe they can identify this common thread. However, the attempt to state in propositional terms what this common core actually is leads to a fundamental difficulty: 'Because this core experience is said to be common to a wide diversity of religions, it is difficult or impossible to specify its distinctive features, and yet unless this is done, the assertion of commonality becomes logically and empirically vacuous.'[30]

It is impossible to state what this common experience actually is, because one has to use the concepts and vocabulary of a particular tradition. The tradition of liberalism supplies suitably vague categories in order to attempt to be neutral in its description of religious experience. Using these vague categories to cover all the varied details of specific traditions makes it difficult, perhaps impossible, to find evidence that could ever count against the liberal claim. There are no conflicting truth claims or creedal statements that can contradict the pluralist claim of a common religious experience. This is

---

[30] Lindbeck, *Doctrine*, 32.

because the claim does not arise as a conclusion of investigation, but is an assumption built into the investigation from the very start. The evidence is always being reinterpreted in terms of the pluralist framework. This makes the pluralist hypothesis hard to contradict. At the level of description, any contradiction between religions can be resolved once this methodological commitment has been made.

There are many further problems with an expressivist approach to religion. By considering Lindbeck's own account a little more it will be possible to identify what they are. I shall also demonstrate that the weakness of theological pluralism lies in the very way that it attempts to describe and explain the world religions. While Hick attempts to describe religions with a view not dependent on any tradition, he fails – his position is as much part of a tradition of enquiry as any other. Furthermore, this tradition of enquiry can only provide an impoverished and reductionist account of the world religions.

Chapter 8

A Religion for the Modern World

Since the Enlightenment, philosophers and theologians have often been driven by the conviction that it is possible to describe and evaluate knowledge from a neutral vantage point. The attempt has been to stand back, as it were, from specific traditions of enquiry in favour of an unbiased viewpoint from which to survey competing claims. From such a vantage point, Hick both surveys the world religions and offers the pluralist hypothesis, a theory of religion that claims to be independent of any specific religious allegiance. But we have identified reasons to question such a claim: although it is true that the pluralist hypothesis does not depend, in Hick's form, upon any one of the major world religions – Christianity, Judaism, Islam, Buddhism or Hinduism – it does not follow that the hypothesis has no religious allegiance. The tradition from which pluralism springs is the ethical religion of Kantianism. As George Lindbeck has argued, this tradition has given rise to the experiential-expressive theologies of liberalism. In this chapter we shall survey further objections to that framework, objections that will go to the heart of the case for religious pluralism.

Individualism

Experiential-expressivism is committed to a highly individualist account of knowledge. This either follows from or gives rise to individualism as a key value for those in the liberal tradition. Given the turn to the subject found in Descartes and modified by Kant, the modern western world continues this deeply individualistic commitment. However, when applied to the interpretation of religion, such individualism leads our interpretations astray.

According to expressivists, the truth value of religious doctrines can only be tested in terms of how well they express the inner experience of believers. For example, Hick claims that the test of many crucial doctrines does not lie in some correspondence theory of truth, but 'in the appropriateness to the myth's referent of the behavioural dispositions it tends to evoke in the hearer'.[1] The mistake in this approach lies in its illusory attempt to 'locate ultimately significant contact with whatever is finally important to religion in the prereflective experiential depths of the self'.[2] The attempt is mistaken because a religious tradition is not the product of individuals who come to believe as a result of their own personal feelings. Religion, as any empirical study will show, is a communal affair. People belong to communities or traditions in which their experience is formed. Far from being secondary, the doctrines of a tradition shape the experience of its members.

Lindbeck develops his own radical view of the communitarian context of religion in contrast to a cognitive-realist view of doctrine. This is a weakness in his position, which cannot explain how beliefs ever begin.[3] If doctrines always determine the experience of believers and never arise from them, then one must ask how those doctrinal convictions initially arise. Without an answer to this question there is no way of explaining the origins of religion. Indeed, one is left with the feeling that Lindbeck is engaged in his own form of reductionism. While the expressivists reduce doctrine to an experiential component, Lindbeck reduces doctrine to its function within a community or tradition. Nonetheless, the criticism of expressivism embedded in his alternative account remains powerful and helpful.

Religion and Community

Lindbeck's proposal for understanding doctrine describes religion as a cultural-linguistic framework. This framework is the

---

[1] Hick, *An Interpretation of Religion*, 348.
[2] Lindbeck, *The Nature of Doctrine*, 21.
[3] This argument is very helpfully made in McGrath, *The Genesis of Doctrine*, 14–34.

objective collection of customs, rituals and language that shape the way men and women live, think and feel. For this reason, doctrine is given a place prior to experience: 'it is a common phenomenon that shapes the subjectivities of individuals rather than being a manifestation of those subjectivities'.[4] By this reversal of the relationship between inner experience and religious belief, Lindbeck overcomes certain failings in expressivism. His approach does not share the radical individualism of expressivism, nor its anti-doctrinal commitment: trying to get 'behind' doctrines to something else. The tradition of enquiry to which believers belong is taken seriously as the source of religious experience; and the implication for theological pluralism is devastating: 'Adherents of different religions do not diversely thematize the same experience; rather they have different experiences.'[5] Religious doctrines, scriptures, histories and creeds must be taken seriously as the only possible access to the claimed religious experience of believers. Far from trying to crush inter-religious dialogue, Lindbeck presents this framework as a more stable platform for such encounters. The starting point for encounter between the adherents of diverse religions should lie in a comparison of what they actually say and believe, rather than in a theoretical perspective that attempts to systematise all apparent rivals into one coherent narrative: 'They can regard themselves as simply different and can proceed to explore their agreements and disagreements without necessarily engaging in the invidious comparisons that the assumption of a common experiential core make so tempting.'[6]

Expressivism leads such encounters astray because it presumes to know what lies at the heart of the dialogue partner's religion even before any conversation has begun. Lindbeck offers a basis

---

[4] Lindbeck, *Doctrine*, 33.

[5] Lindbeck, *Doctrine*, 40.

[6] Lindbeck, *Doctrine*, 55. The characteristics of a postliberal approach to dialogue is discussed in DiNoia, 'Varieties of Religious Aims: Beyond Exclusivism, Inclusivism, and Pluralism' in Marshall (ed.), *Theology and Dialogue*. A postliberal approach to apologetics is discussed in Kamitsuka, 'The Justification of Religious Belief in the Pluralist Public Realm: Another Look at Postliberal Apologetics', 588–606.

for a true form of pluralism in contrast to the underlying monism of Hick's account. Nonetheless, it remains a weakness in Lindbeck's position that he dispenses with cognitive realism. Doing so confuses what it would mean for Christianity (or any other religion) to be true. His motivation for this omission is the desire to avoid bringing any neutral categories into the debate. To use 'truth' as defined by realists suggests a concept distinct from Christianity to which Christians must subscribe. Lindbeck believes all truth to be intra-systematic. That is, truth for a Christian means something distinct from truth for a Buddhist.

Truth Testing

Though there is a potential weakness at this point in Lindbeck's work, there is also a great strength in his approach to doctrine. Lindbeck claims that if one wishes to test the truth of Christianity in contrast to other religions, one cannot proceed in terms of individual doctrines (there being no neutral rule to decide between them), but only in terms of doctrines as part of a tradition. That tradition, as a whole, should be seen as a 'gigantic proposition'.[7] For example, the Christian doctrine of the Trinity cannot be tested by standards of empiricism or Aristotelian logic alone; it can only be tested as part of a gigantic proposition: the Christian tradition, including Christology, pneumatology, the doctrines of revelation, language, ontology, and so on. The truthfulness of Christianity stands or falls as a whole.

The theological pluralist pays no heed to this homogenous sense in which doctrines belong to the traditions of which they are a part. This leads them into a serious fallacy. For example, Lindbeck concedes that 'all religions recommend something which can be called "love"', but he points out that this 'is a banality as uninteresting as the fact that all languages are (or were) spoken'.[8] Concepts, doctrines, ethics, and so on, cannot be isolated from the tradition in which they are given: 'The significant things are the distinctive patterns of story, belief, ritual, and

---

[7] Lindbeck, *Doctrine*, 51.
[8] Lindbeck, *Doctrine*, 42.

behaviour that give "love" and "God" their specific and sometimes contradictory meanings.'[9] This fallacy goes to the heart of
Hick's pluralism. His attempt to interpret religion in terms of his
epistemology leads him to believe that faith can be treated as a
neutral category applicable to all religions. Pursuing this method,
he goes on to analyse morality as a general category too. So it is
that beliefs and behaviour are isolated from their contexts within
a religious tradition, and are harmonised in accordance with his
presupposed common underlying experience.

MacIntyre and Lindbeck represent a postmodern rejection of the
long-established Enlightenment tradition. Both thinkers identify in
modernism a failure to take seriously the communal nature of belief
that arises from the simple fact that believers belong to traditions of
enquiry. From Descartes to Hick the modern west has been spell-
bound by the Copernican revolution, whose turn from outside
authority to the autonomy of the subject has been the key theme
over the last two centuries. Now there is a major cultural shift away
from this approach. Lacking among the postmodernists is a strong
sense of the cognitive significance of doctrine, and here a properly
biblical theology must distinguish itself from postmodern theology.
Nonetheless, the postmodern critique reveals the true hollowness
of theological pluralism. In the following chapter I shall level a
central charge of this book against Hick's theological pluralism: its
implicit atheism. But first, the postliberal charge can be focused in
terms of how it would apply to Hick's treatment of religious
language.

In keeping with the work of Kant and Schleiermacher, Hick
must interpret the bulk of religious language as second-order sym-
bolism and yet, in keeping with his own claims to realism, he must
also maintain certain cognitive religious claims. Yet Kant has
already set the trajectory for Hick's work. The expressivist approach
to religion always eats up religious realism, its concern with imma-
nent reality eclipsing any vestige of transcendent reality. Whether in
ethics or experience, religion is inevitably reduced to a component
of human psychology. I shall now unpack this movement in Hick's
philosophy of language.

---

[9] Lindbeck, *Doctrine*, 42.

Language and Truth

Hick has emphasised certain literary forms in the course of his work without devoting a great deal of space to discussing the exact sense in which he uses them. We may briefly trace his use of the terms 'myth' and 'metaphor' through his work to gain a basic understanding of what he means by them. He has consistently claimed that religion is essentially fact asserting; he distances his own position from the non-realism of Don Cupitt. However, not all religious truth claims can be understood as simple assertions of fact. If they were, then the pluralist hypothesis would be impossible: too many obviously contradictory doctrines exist among the religions of the world. Hick's account of religious language allows him to distinguish between language that is fact asserting and language that has a different function.

While in his early work Hick establishes the basic fact-asserting nature of religion, his thought leaves 'ample scope for the non-factual language of myth, symbol and poetry to express the believer's awareness of the illimitable mysteries which surround that core of religious fact'.[10] Hick means by mysteries those many areas of religious belief where there are gaps in our knowledge. These gaps are filled by myths and poetry. The relationship of myths to literal language is one of supplement and adornment; they are imaginary, non-cognitive expressions, which adorn the essential facts of religious belief. If all religious language were interpreted as myth, then Hick declares we would not come up with a revision of Christianity so much as an obituary for it. Therefore, the basic, realist conviction that God exists was offered in Hick's early work as a non-negotiable literal use of language.

The line between myth and literal language changes in the course of Hick's work, but not the basic dichotomy itself. In his contribution to *The Myth of God Incarnate* Hick builds on the work of his fellow contributors to describe the mythological value of a high Christology. He declares that the claim 'the historical Jesus of Nazareth was also God is as devoid of meaning as to say that this circle drawn with a pencil on paper is also a square'.[11] Any statement

---

[10] Hick, *God and the Universe of Faiths*, 22–3.

[11] Hick, 'Jesus and the World Religions' in Hick (ed.), *The Myth of God Incarnate*, 178.

that is a contradiction in terms, an exaggeration, illogical or other-wise meaningless, cannot be taken seriously as a literal claim. Instead, such language is to be construed as mythological: 'a myth is a story which is told but which is not literally true, or an idea or image which is applied to someone or something but which does not literally apply, but which invites a particular attitude in its hearers'.[12]

Hick is not using myth here to mean a fable or mistake. Myth has a positive value. Nor need myth always mean a story – a non-narra-tive concept or doctrine might be a myth. What defines a myth is that it does not make a literal claim about an objective reality that could be tested by some form of the correspondence theory of truth. Rather, a myth is a functional use of language designed to evoke a certain form of behaviour. The appropriate truth test for a myth lies in examining the kind of behaviour it inspires in believers.

Hick provides a more sustained treatment of the myth/literal distinction in *An Interpretation of Religion*, where he states once again the familiar distinction with its appropriate truth tests. A belief is lit-eral if the truth test that it requires 'consists in its conformity or lack of conformity to fact'. But a myth does not have this literal intent; it 'tends to evoke an appropriate dispositional attitude',[13] and this function must be tested by alternative criteria. Hick does not pursue his account of myth in terms of a literary type, only in terms of its function in language use. This explains why he easily slips between using the word 'myth' and using the word 'metaphor'. No differ-ence of any significance is implied in his use of either word despite their significantly different use in literature. For Hick, any concept that serves this function may be identified as a myth or a metaphor. His loose definition allows him to treat both the story of the fall in the Garden of Eden and the doctrine of transubstantiation as mythologies. Hick produces an argument in which metaphor, anal-ogy, allegory, parable, and even interpreted history, are rolled into one under the general category of 'myth'. He gives an example of a myth by describing a devious committee meeting as 'the work of the devil'.[14] This seems to be an obvious example of a metaphor,

---

[12] Hick, 'Jesus', 178.

[13] Hick, *Interpretation*, 348.

[14] Hick, *Interpretation*, 348.

but, in accordance with Hick's non-technical use of linguistic terms, he describes it as a myth. The unfortunate result of this unnuanced account is that it produces a framework in which only two language types are possible. There is literal-factual language and non-literal mythological language. All language use has to be squeezed into one or other of these categories.

Sensitive to some of these criticisms, Hick has more recently given a little qualification to his claims. While still maintaining that all myth can be reduced to its literal meaning, he now admits that some loss is entailed. Using the example of how the word 'plough-ing' may be used metaphorically, he says that 'we must note that ploughing may have partially different associations for different people, so that the statement may evoke a range of differing responses. This openness of the web of associations prevents meta-phors from being definitively translated into literal terms, for we cannot limit their field of possible associations.'[15]

This is as far as Hick will go in recognising the rich dimensions of language. As if he has almost opened a door only to close it again, he then affirms, 'It is a mistake to think – as many vaguely do – that myths can express deep truths that cannot be expressed in any other way.'[16] Myth and metaphor remain embellishments to the literal truth claims at the heart of religion. This account employs the leading assumptions of the modernist movement: there are general, universal categories of language and reason in terms of which all the diversity of religions and traditions may be interpreted and described. Whether we are discussing Hinduism, Shinto, or Southern Baptist Christianity, any truth claims that are not readily amenable to a certain type of correspondence truth test are treated together as myths.[17] The remaining literal claims are those that may be tested by the standards of empiricism – claims concerning sense experience. These standards are sup-posed to be independent of any particular tradition and permit the dissection of all religions into their literal and non-literal

---

[15] Hick, *The Fifth Dimension*, 230.

[16] Hick, *Dimension*, 230–31.

[17] Harold Netland provides a very informative discussion of the direct way in which the otherwise profoundly contrasting traditions of Christianity and Shinto are in intellectual conflict *Dissonant Voices*, 93–111.

elements. Here is the encyclopaedist vision in its late twentieth-century form.

Language and Myth

Hick's dualist account of language echoes the dualism implicit in his Kantian epistemology, the radical distinction between two components ruling out hybrid forms of experience and language use. But this is a clumsy approach to the richness of theological language. For example, Marshall describes the relationship between myth and truth as something that can only be settled on a case by case basis: 'To say that a story is a myth is not to pronounce on its historical truth or falsity . . . A myth may or may not employ historical materials.'[18] Hick defines myth in such a way that he must pronounce on its falsity a priori. Myths are simply not true – only the kernel of literal truth, which may in some cases be extracted, can be described as true. Gillis points out the poverty of this approach: 'what is not obvious, or at least not to Hick, is that metaphor discloses or reveals truth, and that it does so precisely in its form as metaphor. It does not refer to or rely upon any other language structure to do so.'[19]

There are two types of myth according to Hick's account. The first of these are expository myths, which attempt to express a basic truth about human existence in imaginative terms. They can be reduced to literal terms with loss only to their emotive impact. Hick is quite optimistic that we can extract all we need from such narratives. For example, the story of the fall in the Garden of Eden is simply an ornamental way of telling us 'the fact that ordinary human life is lived in alienation from God and hence from one's neighbours and from the natural environment'.[20] This example brings to light the poverty of Hick's account of language. Firstly, there is the problem of his drastic selectivity in such a supposedly definitive interpretation of the Genesis story. Secondly, there is the underlying problem that Hick is guilty, on his own terms, of simply substituting one myth for another.

---

[18] Marshall, 'Myth' in Ferguson and Wright (eds.), *New Dictionary of Theology*, 450.
[19] Gillis, *A Question of Final Belief*, 165.
[20] Hick, *Interpretation*, 349.

Consider Hick's 'non-mythical' account of the fall. The concept of 'ordinary' human life, the meaning of 'alienation', the supposed relationships to God, others and the environment are far from being simple, literal statements. Surely a relationship to the environment is parasitic on the notion of a relationship to other people? And if we concede that this is a metaphor, then does that not demand that we continue stripping away such mythological garb in order to get to the irreducible core? This process must continue in regard to almost every element in the story. Indeed, not only the fall but every claim about God is subjected to this treatment. This is as profound a problem in Hick's system as it had been for Kant: what kind of God is really left when this demythologising process reaches its conclusion? This problem becomes more acute with reference to the second type of myth.

The second type of myth deals with ultimate mysteries that are described by using analogies, not stories. To say 'God is wise' is an example of this type of myth. It is a way of speaking directly about something of which we cannot speak. This is a useful device for maintaining the pluralist hypothesis in the face of apparent contradictions. Hick's epistemic framework draws a sharp line between the Real as we know it and the Real *an sich*, and this type of myth must be used in our frail attempts to describe the Real. Consider the following account of what we are able to say of the Real *an sich*: 'Thus it cannot be said to be one or many, person or thing, substance or process, good or evil, purposive or non-purposive. None of the concrete descriptions that apply within the realm of human experience can apply literally to the unexperiencable ground of that realm.'[21]

There are two problems this view presents for religious knowledge. Firstly, there are cognitive limits in our experience of Ultimate Reality. Secondly, there are the limitations of language itself as a vehicle to describe that experience. Indeed, the existence of the Real is no more than a postulate of religious experience; it is not something we have direct access to. The language we use to describe the Real is mythological: 'None of the descriptive terms that apply within the realm of human experience can apply literally

---

[21] Hick, *Interpretation*, 246.

to the unexperiencable reality that underlies that realm.'[22] This second use of mythological language is simply our way of speaking about something we cannot speak of, and therefore the language does not apply to the supposed reality itself. Of course, Hick continues to affirm religious realism, but it is a seriously truncated form of realism.

What is objectively claimed by our religious language use is twofold. Firstly, that there is an Ultimate Reality that exists and, secondly, that human life offers limitlessly good possibilities. The remaining religious language use is mythological and does not actually apply to transcendent reality. To what then does it apply? Myth applies to the Real's 'phenomenal manifestations'.[23] This is the heart of Hick's analysis of religious language. We are not really talking about Ultimate Reality at all. We are only ever talking about the phenomenal appearances of that Real. Mythology is the essential form of almost all religious language.

When one analyses religious language in terms of Hick's framework, only a few, purely formal, claims still apply to the Real: the bulk of our language describes only our own images of the Real. These myths can themselves be reduced to a core, literal, content. This content does not disclose anything about the Real, only about how we should behave. Hick claims that all true myths serve to guide our response to the Real by evoking in us the appropriate behaviour. Expository myths, like the story of the fall, can be reduced to a literal statement about human existence with loss only to its emotive impact. The second type of myth cannot be reduced to something else because its meaning is identical to its emotive impact. To lose the emotive impact of 'God is wise' is to lose its very meaning. In fact, when the expository myth has been demythologised one tends to be left with a myth of this second type. For example, Hick classifies the doctrine of transubstantiation as an expository myth that serves to occasion 'special openness to God as known through Christ'.[24] However, the expressions 'God as known through Christ' or even 'openness to God' fail, in Hick's account, to be literal claims. Like the use of alienation in Hick's analysis of the

---

[22] Hick, *Interpretation*, 350.
[23] Hick, *Interpretation*, 351.
[24] Hick, *Interpretation*, 349.

fall, such phrases only describe how believers respond to and feel about the 'phenomenal manifestations' of the Real. Their meaning lies in the impact they have on a believer's attitudes and lifestyle. Therefore, such expository myths boil down to the second form of myth, and there is really only this one use of myth underlying all Hick's analysis. Myths are forms of language use that serve to affect our behaviour. They cannot tell us anything about the Real in itself, which is beyond both understanding and description.

Hick reads his understanding of myth back into the history of religious development. He claims that religious language was never primarily about offering metaphysical descriptions of supernatural reality, but with inspiring certain forms of behaviour. Therefore, religions should never be compared in terms of doctrinal creeds but in terms of the kind of behaviour those creeds inspire. Concerning the most diverse religions, eastern and western, Hick concludes, 'it may well be that their differing eschatological mythologies serve the same soteriological function'.[25] Hick finds evidential support for his argument in the apparent similarities among the religions in the type of moral 'fruit' they tend to produce; and there are common characteristics shared by great religious leaders in all the major religious traditions. Hick is able to make this connection without worrying about the otherwise obvious contradictions of their beliefs, because of his treatment of language as myth. Any doctrines that, taken literally, would tend to cause division are relativised in favour of their functional value.

If religious language is mostly myth, then there is little importance to attach to any conflicting truth claims. In any case, Hick argues that there are few clearly contradictory doctrines, and that most contradictions are only apparent. There are three types of contradiction that Hick deals with. Firstly, there are contradictory beliefs about *historical facts* (did Jesus die on the cross or was it, as the Qu'ran suggests, only someone who looked like Jesus?). Secondly, there are contradictory claims about *trans-historical ideas* such as the nature of life after death. Thirdly, there are contradictory pictures or images of what the *Ultimate Reality* is like.

Only the first type of contradiction may be tested by certain, agreed methods of investigation. In principle, given enough data, it

---

[25] Hick, *Interpretation*, 356.

might be possible to distinguish true from false beliefs regarding historical events. However, Hick denies this will happen in practice. How could we ever be certain that we have enough data to bring an absolute verdict? Therefore we must suspend judgement on disagreements over historic events. The second type of contradiction cannot be settled by any known methods of investigation. Descriptions of creation or eschatology are beyond present examination. The only test possible is the pragmatic question of what impact they have on our present lives. Do they generate moral behaviour? The third type of contradiction involves a language use that can never be truly contradictory, because it is never actually literal. Such language describes our response to an infinite reality. Given an infinite variety of possible manifestations of that reality, of course there will be some that appear contradictory.

This analysis of religious language in terms of myth is a process of setting aside cultural and historical peculiarities of religion in favour of a supposed universal significance. No matter what religious practitioners might say, Hick is able to demythologise their beliefs such that there is no final contradiction with the beliefs of others. Hick belongs to the modernist tradition of seeking a common, universal language in which the real content of religions can be expressed and harmonised. It is not surprising that the resulting core of religion is found to be its ethical significance. This is just as Kant said it would be.

A Universal Language for Religion

Hick has always shared with the Kantian tradition a commitment to a universal rational and moral framework for the interpretation and evaluation of religion. From his doctoral dissertation to his present work, Hick has been convinced that it is possible to describe an epistemology independent of any particular tradition. In the terms of this epistemology any religious belief can be analysed and assessed. This commitment leads him quite naturally from offering his epistemology originally as an account of Christian belief to offering it as an interpretation of religious belief in general. Hick is continuing the modernist project of undermining the relevance of tradition-specific enquiry in favour of a neutral account of religious knowledge. He prefers the view from nowhere: no external authority, nor historical contingencies, shape Hick's view of religion. Rather, he is guided by what he considers the universal principles of morality and faith.

Hick's three-step progressive epistemology is the exact reverse of MacIntyre's own 'tradition constituted' view of enquiry. For Hick, knowledge begins with a natural sense of the universe and leads to a religious interpretation through a moral perspective on life. MacIntyre demonstrates that the religious perspective is foundational and provided by the tradition to which one already belongs. This gives the context in which one can make sense of life. A tradition provides both a moral framework for making decisions and a basic outlook on the nature of reality. Whether the world is created or eternal, real or illusory, are all important, theological questions; and our answers to these questions shape our view of reality. No doubt, for most people those answers are held implicitly rather than being consciously chosen because they pick them up through the culture in which they grow up. Nonetheless, it is the tradition that is shaping the scientific and moral conclusions of the individual. In contrast, Hick offers an individualist approach to knowledge. We, the individual subjects, are masters of all knowledge. We interpret the natural world the way we do for subjective reasons and the same can be said for moral and religious knowledge. Personal feelings and experience guide our interpretations of the world around, and what we think about a religious or secular tradition is dependent on this personal outlook.

Is Hick mistaken? Certainly, the postmodern rediscovery of the role of community would suggest so. Lindbeck and MacIntyre share a sense that the cultural and linguistic community of which we are a part shape our outlook in a significant way. Indeed, there really is no 'world' other than the world that is already interpreted through the tradition of which we are a part; and the language in which we describe the 'world' is not reducible to some neutral, literal language. The mistake of Hick and the modernists is to privilege one mode of discourse – the scientific language of empiricism and positivism – over all others. This is why, for Hick, myth and metaphor are largely redundant forms of speech. The pluralist proposal is offered as a literal interpretation of what religion really means; and the cultural peculiarities of religions merely form the optional, mythological garb.

Hick shares in a classical approach to metaphor with roots in the work of Aristotle, who is understood to have described metaphor as 'one of the means of giving decorous "effect" to speech'.[26] Metaphor was simply treated as an expendable ornamentation to otherwise literal language use,[27] and the purpose of that metaphor was largely for emotive effect. This reductionism is evident in Hick's three-step epistemology. The third step, religious interpretation, is simply a total explanation of the previous two steps – the natural and the moral. Therefore, there is no new knowledge added by the step of religious interpretation. The only addition is a way of explaining the previous two steps. Consequently, the literal core of religious language is restricted to those elements that refer either to the natural world (such as the historicity of Jesus) or to moral affairs (such as the categorical imperative or golden rule). Religious language does not refer to some extra 'things' that have not already been expressed in those former two levels, because such language is utterly dependent on the former two steps.

So religious language may be expressed in moral or natural terms at a cost to its emotive value, but not to its literal sense. Of course, Hick would claim that religious experience is the added dimension of knowledge in the third epistemological step. However, the experience itself is simply psychological – something that can be entirely explained in natural, literal language. The claim that religious experience has an object is no more than a postulate. It is not a new component of knowledge, but only a way of explaining our psychological experience. All language can be explained in these natural, non-supernatural, terms, even though, as Hick argues, such postulates are entirely reasonable. Therefore, religious experience adds no new information to what was already known by natural and moral reasoning.

Janet Martin Soskice has given ample demonstration that such a reductionist approach to metaphor is seriously flawed. Metaphors are essential in all forms of discourse, though perhaps especially useful in religious language. Metaphors are irreducible because they

---

[26] Hawkes, *Metaphor*, 11.
[27] Gillis, *Question*, 141–3.

always have a relationship to a wide range of related metaphors, which cannot simply be defined in non-metaphorical terms. For example, to say 'God is my Rock' is to relate God to a whole realm of ideas and cross-references within the network of biblical and non-biblical imagery. Instead of a reductionist approach, Soskice argues that metaphors form part of a model for understanding reality – to reduce metaphors to something else is to destroy that model altogether. She summarises her own argument against reductionism in the following way:

> We have said that criticisms of metaphor in religious language often conceal a more radical critique of the possibility of any talk of God, of any traditional theologizing at all. This is so because the traditional empiricist criticisms of 'non-literal' speech are … in the end, attacks on the possibility of any metaphysics. The plan of our counter-argument has been to show that models and metaphysical theory terms may, in both the scientific and religious cases, be reality depicting without pretending to be directly descriptive, and by doing so to support the Christian's right to make metaphysical claims.[28]

Soskice is able to draw upon parallels with the use of metaphor in science to make her claim. Although scientific language is sometimes held up as the great example of literal language use, many scientists recognise the crucial value of metaphor and model in scientific theory, discovery and communication. Ian Barbour argues that metaphor is an essential, irreducible element in scientific discourse. He asserts that 'a metaphor cannot be replaced by a set of literal statements' because it is, by nature, 'open-ended'.[29] The use of metaphors implies that we need to stretch language in order to understand reality more satisfactorily. Whether in science or religion, metaphors are essential if we are to attempt a description of the true nature of reality. If this means that our language is 'stretched', then that only indicates the wonderful, mind-bending, dimensions of our universe. Hick's attempt to demythologise religion reveals very clearly the poverty of a modernist approach to language: God becomes the insipid 'Ultimate Real'; the acts of repentance and

---

[28] Soskice, *Metaphor and Religious Language*, 145.
[29] Barbour, Myths, Models and Paradigms, 14.

faith become the turn from 'self-centredness to Reality-centredness'. The vague literal words into which Hick translates rich religious terms do not simply lack emotive impact; they also lack descriptive content. This is inevitable because Hick does not really see religious language in descriptive terms. For him, religious language does not describe a reality 'out there', but only our inner feelings and emotions.

We have seen in this chapter the wider modernist worldview of which Hick is a part. From Kant and Schleiermacher to the present day there are theologians who have identified a literal core of religion and dispensed with the rest as culturally conditioned. Religious pluralism is the natural consequence of this identification. Whether in matters of morality or experience, such a vague, neutral core is compatible with any religion. But in the attempt to arrive at this core, modernism has also revealed its incoherence. It is incoherent because it is simply smuggling in its own metaphors and privileged language use at the expense of a truly religious framework. Furthermore, it is impossible to escape metaphor, myth and model in religious discourse.

The entire methodology Hick is using also rests on switching one source of authority for another. Instead of submitting claims to church traditions, councils or divine revelation, Hick prefers the authoritative voice of Enlightenment rationality. This alternative system of authority is a poor alternative for anyone wishing to profess a Christian faith. Granting a particular tradition of human reason final authority for what is true and about what we can speak produces only an emaciated religion. This is what we find in Hick's interpretation of religion, as we shall see in the next chapter. Pluralism brings the modernist project of Kant not only to a logical conclusion, but also to a bankrupt one. At the centre of Hick's universe of faiths lie neither God nor the Real, but an empty space: there is nothing at the centre of the universe of faiths but our own self.

Chapter 9

The Unknown God of Pluralism

In this survey of the philosophical background to Hick's theology of religious pluralism it has been argued that he is thoroughly committed to a modernist understanding of religion. Hick owes his own philosophical Copernican revolution to the tradition articulated supremely by Kant. This revolution, often referred to as the 'turn to the self', places the human knower as not only the starting point for philosophy (a step with which the earlier philosopher, Descartes, would have been happy), but also as the object of philosophy. It is the human knower, with all his or her limitations, who is both the arbiter of knowledge and the object of knowledge. This turn to the self sits uneasily with the theology of Kant, whose rhetorical commitment to a broadly Christian framework can seem hard to reconcile with his philosophy. However, as we have already noted, his theological thought may never have been more than a halfway house to a thoroughly secular philosophy – a transcendent God is of no ultimate necessity to Kant's theology other than as a postulate for morality.

Hick's theology draws out the consequences of this quasi-secular philosophy. One particular religious doctrine trimmed and, eventually, excluded from his thought, is the doctrine of revelation. Hick's work gives little evidence of a proper concept of divine revelation, an omission shared by the work of Kant. The possibility of revelation in the strong sense of a declaration from God providing knowledge otherwise unavailable to the human subject is alien to the philosophy of the Enlightenment. This follows naturally from the modernist antipathy to any concept of a God who speaks. We shall first establish the extent to which revelation plays any part in Hick's thought and then consider what this implies for his pluralist case.

Avery Dulles provides a helpful typology for understanding the various ways Christians have tried to describe divine revelation. In his outline of five models of revelation, Dulles identifies Hick as a possible proponent of two of them. This apparent ambivalence reflects an underlying confusion in Hick's own position. He certainly wants to retain some notion of revelation, and so pays lip-service to revelatory language. However, despite this use of orthodox language his philosophy compels him to dispense with any such notion. Though it may appear that Hick's work could fit into two of the following models of revelation, in fact it fits into none of them.

Model 1: Doctrinal Propositional

The first model is doctrinal. Proponents of this position would include evangelicals and conservative Catholics. Characteristic of this model is a description of revelation in two forms: *general* (natural) and *special* (supernatural). General revelation provides men and women with a partial knowledge of God through reason, conscience and the natural order. Special revelation involves some kind of miraculous verbal communication from God. While evangelicals locate this special revelation in Scripture, conservative Catholics identify a double source in both the Bible and tradition. Dulles, himself a Catholic, criticises this model for being 'highly authoritarian' and not 'favourable to dialogue with other churches and religions'.[1] Hick also identifies and rejects this model of revelation in his treatment of the Thomist-Catholic model of faith. Clearly Hick never intended to promote the doctrinal propositional model of revelation. We have already had reason to question his brief dismissal of propositional knowledge, and the questions then raised also apply to his dismissal of propositional revelation.

Model 2: Revelation as History

There is overlap between the first model and the second in the importance of written documents. In this model God is seen as

---

[1] Dulles, *Models of Revelation*, 50–51.

revealing himself through significant events in history. We primarily know of these events only through the written witness of Scripture. For Dulles, Oscar Cullman provides just such a mediating position. Though he affirms the priority of events over their interpretation, he still maintains that those interpretative records are essential if we are to have any access to revelation. Therefore, God has revealed himself through historical events, but these would be unknown to us if not for the historical records of Scripture. Without the Scriptures those events could not count as revelatory. Wolfhart Pannenberg, in contrast, offers a more strictly non-propositional account of revelation through history, where the events interpret themselves and do not require an independent interpretation for them to count as revelatory. This permits Pannenberg to develop a significantly universal account of revelation: 'Revelation, he holds, is not to be found in a special segment of history but rather in universal history – the history of the whole world as it moves to its appointed consummation.'[2]

Pannenberg's form of the revelation-through-history model would be more conducive to a pluralist view than the account given by Cullman.[3] However, the shared feature of this model is a characteristic incompatible with Hick's epistemology. This model assumes that a historical event might itself be revelatory, whereas Hick argues that historical events, in themselves, are always fundamentally ambiguous. For example, in words that might suggest the revelation-as-history model, he claims, 'Jeremiah was conscious of the downfall of the kingdom in the seventh century BCE as God's just disciplining of the erring Israelites'.[4] However, as a matter of historical fact, Hick notes that nothing more has happened than Israel being invaded by a more powerful foreign army. The religious dimension of the event does not lie in the historical incident but in the subjective interpretation arising from a special kind of experience of the event (religious seeing-as). This suggests that

---

[2] Dulles, *Models*, 59.

[3] It is important to note that Pannenberg himself is highly critical of John Hick's pluralism; 'Religious Pluralism and Conflicting Truth Claims' in D'Costa (ed.), *Christian Uniqueness Reconsidered*, 96–106.

[4] Hick, *An Interpretation of Religion*, 155.

Hick might be more comfortable with the third model of revelation.

Model 3: Revelation as Inner Experience

The third account departs entirely from the objective sense of revelation present in the first two models. In this model revelation is described as a personal experience of individuals in the form of a mystical encounter rather than as a spoken word or public event. Dulles describes Karl Rahner as representative of this position. For Rahner 'revelation initially occurs in a mysterious experience with God, called in his system "transcendental revelation"'.[5] Theologians who use this model view revelation not as the communication of objective truths, but as an encounter with a person. Dulles identifies Auguste Sabatier, a French liberal Protestant, as a proponent of this model. Sabatier was himself influenced by the foundational work of Schleiermacher who is a classic example of a theologian committed to the primacy of inner experience. Schleiermacher describes 'a consciousness of God' which may 'be really a revelation' because revelation is a matter of inner experience rather than objective words or event.[6]

Those who use this model point to the prophets as examples of people who had a profound experience of personal familiarity with God. No distinction is made between the revelation given and the personal response to that revelation. The personal, subjective feeling of response to the divine is itself the revelation. Given the similarities between Hick and Schleiermacher it is not surprising that Dulles identifies Hick as a proponent of this model: 'The great founders of religions, he [Hick] holds, are persons on whose consciousness the Transcendent has impinged in new ways with special intensity and power. Since the same infinite Spirit presses in continually on every individual, it is possible, Hick contends, for others to find meaning and credibility in what the mystics claim to have experienced.'[7]

---

[5] Dulles, *Models*, 70.
[6] Schleiermacher, *The Christian Faith*, 52.
[7] Dulles, *Models*, 70.

This characterisation of Hick's work emphasises the important theme of the universality of religious experience. In keeping with the philosophy of Kant, Hick shares basic convictions that whatever religious experience is, it must be something universally accessible, and that universal experience is itself the divine revelation. Given that religious experience is universal, it follows that revelation is universal: it is available at all times and in all places where there are human beings willing to see things that way. This seems to be a fitting account of Hick's position, but, given that Dulles also describes his work as an example of the fifth model, it is an account we shall have to review. Before we turn to that final model, let us briefly consider the fourth model.

Model 4: The Dialectical Model of Revelation

The fourth model is that of revelation as a dialectical presence and is foundational to three of the great German theologians: Barth, Brunner and Bultmann. Proponents of this model locate revelation in an event that is neither an objective 'thing' (such as the Bible or a historical event), nor a subjective happening (such as inner illumination). Neither way of locating revelation takes seriously enough divine sovereignty. In contrast, the dialectical model describes objective factors, such as Scripture, as only witnesses to revelation. Revelation itself is a dialectical event of God's self-disclosure creating its own response in the recipient. The problem with the former models of revelation we have considered is that they try to describe revelation in isolation from the divine will. Yet any attempt to describe revelation as something separable from the divine will must fail. Such descriptions cannot really be anything more than descriptions of human things. The dialectical account has given rise to some of the more robust versions of religious exclusivism.[8] Revelation is identified with Christ as God's self-disclosure and in the dialectical encounter with Christ. Such an absolute identification seems to destroy the possibility of any universally available revelation. It is not surprising that Karl Barth is often identified as a major

---

[8] E.g., Kraemer, *Religion and the Christian Faith*.

example of an exclusivist theologian.[9] This model is entirely incompatible with Hick's thought.

Model 5: Revelation as New Awareness

The fifth model is distinctive in granting to the human subject a creative role in the process of revelation. Revelation is not something given from the outside by some external being: 'According to this approach revelation is a transcendent fulfilment of the inner drive of the human spirit toward fuller consciousness.'[10] This inner drive is related to human progress and an evolutionary account of human development. Revelation accompanies the progressive evolution of the human faculties. The work of the Roman Catholic theologian, Teilhard de Chardin, is a prime example of a theologian using this model. Like the third model, human experience is the vehicle of revelation; however, it 'finds revelation not in withdrawal from the world but rather in involvement'.[11] It is as men and women interact with their world that they give rise to moments of revelatory experience. The content of revelation does not point to the existence of a divine being distinct from the human race, but rather to self-consciousness as divine. Because revelation is bound up in human consciousness this model leads one to expect universal qualities in human experience. Revelation is not bound by verbal statements or historic events, but is universally accessible as a stage of higher awareness. Dulles identifies Hick as a proponent of this model, noting that his 'recognition of revelation in the non-Christian religions rests on the premise that revelation does not essentially consist in doctrine but in encounter and awareness'.[12]

The particular kind of encounter and awareness suggested by the fifth model is a heightened awareness of the significance of our surroundings, rather than a specific inner experience of God. This fits well with Hick's account of faith as the reinterpretation of natural and moral significance. Revelation is left with no fixed content and

---

[9] E.g., Race, *Christians and Religious Pluralism*, 11–17.
[10] Dulles, *Models*, 98.
[11] Dulles, *Models*, 102.
[12] Dulles, *Models*, 107.

is free to revise past beliefs wherever necessary in order to fit in with higher stages of consciousness. This model shares with the third and fourth a sense of the contemporaneous nature of revelation, but, in contrast to them, does not identify any non-subjective source to act as a control over what may count as revelation. The model allows a more free-floating description of revelation. While Dulles treats this model as a further category of Christian theology, it is important to note that it gives no special status to the Christian faith: 'It encourages Christians to believe that their own faith could undergo a further development in the distinction of universality by appreciating the perspectives of other human faiths.'[13]

But it is this very openness that undermines the coherence of this model. For example, a Christian form of the claim might suggest that it is Christ who reveals himself even through the unfolding consciousness of non-Christian people. The pluralist could take the claim further and argue that the unfolding revelation might then lead to serious revision of past ideas – including beliefs regarding the historical Jesus. Therefore, the name 'Christ' becomes, as Dulles' demonstrates, a mere cipher for any advance in the spiritual consciousness of men and women. Even secular concepts and ideas might represent new stages in that growing awareness. The word 'Christ' is no more than a token used by a broad movement of consciousness only loosely related to the historical figure of Jesus. This model of revelation fits well various strands of New Age thought with their theme of developing human awareness proceeding into the future, and their happy revision of any past religious claims in keeping with this theme. Hick's unfolding theology over the years has echoed these New Age themes.

Hick's Model of Revelation

Dulles has provided a helpful framework in which to understand how theologians with a broadly Christian outlook understand and apply the doctrine of revelation. However, there is something vague about where Hick's work might fit into this framework.

---

[13] Dulles, *Models*, 111.

Clearly, he would reject the basic thrust of models one, two and four. In each of these cases he must reject the implicit or explicit way the models make Christian revelation normative. These models are not compatible with religious pluralism because they identify something unique in Christ or Scripture, which then determines their response to other claims to revelation. As we have seen, the pluralist hypothesis depends upon the universal accessibility of revelation through the interpretative faculties of human cognition. For Hick, revelation is not tied to a historical event, but to contemporary mental-spiritual processes. His sympathies would lie with models three and five because they share a concept of revelation as something that arises from the universal religious experience of humankind. However, we shall now see that Dulles is mistaken even to categorise Hick as a proponent of these models. Hick's pluralist hypothesis actually implies that there is no such thing as revelation in any of these senses. While Hick continues to use the language of revelation, and this suggests that he has affinities with certain radical Christian theologians, underlying his own position is a more basic commitment to the impossibility of divine revelation. In maintaining this commitment Hick is simply extending the Enlightenment interpretation of religion instigated by Kant.

Dulles argues that Hick uses a version of the third model: revelation as inner experience. This model draws a distinction between non-propositional and propositional forms of knowledge. The latter form of knowledge is conceptual and may be expressed in verbal ways. The former is personal and relational, not easily expressed in words. Revelation as inner experience is a type of non-propositional knowledge, a model of religious knowledge with which Hick has always aligned himself. His first work, *Faith and Knowledge*, was a defence of this distinction. Revelation is not primarily a declaration from an objective divine being, but is the felt response or awareness of the individual to that divinity. Yet sometimes Hick describes his position in a way that sounds a little like the dialectical fourth model: 'revelation is only real or actual in so far as it *becomes* so by being responded to'.[14] However, the dialectical theologians would maintain both the divine prerogative in the moment of

---

[14] Hick, 'The Outcome: Dialogue into Truth' in Hick (ed.), *Truth and Dialogue*, 145.

revelation and the subjective response. This is the very substance of the dialectic: revelation is both divine disclosure and human response in a dialectical relationship. Hick treats revelation differently by dispensing with the objective pole of that relationship. There is no specific, divine activity that he refers to. Revelation is a constant possibility depending not on divine grace, but only on inner experience. The Kantian commitment to the universal accessibility of religious knowledge is absolutely incompatible with dialectical theology.

Hick's account of the axial age in religious development indicates that he is much closer to the fifth model of revelation. According to this model, revelation is closely allied to the evolution of human consciousness. During the axial age a major threshold in personal awareness was crossed from the identification of self with tribe to the awareness of the individual existence of the self. Pre-axial consciousness failed to distinguish between self and society, while axial consciousness recognised the individual self as part of a web of relationships to other individuals, to society at large, and to a great Other, variously known as God. It is ambiguous in Hick's writing whether the Divine instigated this transitional period or whether it is a natural stage in the evolution of consciousness.[15]

In Hick's early work some of his writing suggests God has an active role in revelation, whether during the axial age or at other times. For example, in *Faith and Knowledge* he asks, 'whether we should not expect God to make his revelation in a single mighty act, rather than to produce a number of different, and therefore presumably partial, revelations'?[16] This way of phrasing the question assumes that revelation is something God 'does' or 'makes'. Hick considers two ways in which God might choose to reveal himself: he might choose to 'make' one universally accessible complete revelation, or he might 'produce' a plurality of partial revelations. At this stage Hick was not defending the pluralist

---

[15] Hick is dependent for this account of history on the work of the German theologian, Karl Jaspers. Jaspers' account certainly gives the impression that a traditional view of God is redundant. Indeed, we are on the verge of a new age, according to Jaspers, as a result of the new approach to science and technology. See Jaspers, *The Origin and Goal of History*, 81–8.

[16] Hick, *Faith and Knowledge*, 136.

hypothesis and yet he is already convinced that the latter option is correct. God seems to have chosen to produce partial, limited revelations over the course of time. Though this fits well with a biblical theology of revelation through history, this is not the reason for Hick's preference. His reason for assuming revelation to be partial and multiple in form is because this account fits best with the moral requirement that faith should be an uncompelled response. Occasional, partial, ambiguous revelations leave the human subject with the moral duty to sift the evidence and come to a personal conclusion on whether there is a religious significance to the universe. A single, complete revelation would not offer such ambiguity. Perhaps, then, the axial age was simply a prolonged period of the divine Being giving partial revelation across the cultures of that age? While this is possible, it is significant that the word 'revelation' is absent in his later account of the axial period, as found in *An Interpretation of Religion*.[17] Revelation as an active work of the divine Being was never really compatible with Hick's belief in the radical religious ambiguity of the universe, and so it is quietly dropped in his later writing. This reflects the superfluous nature of the concept in Hick's work. For example, in *The Fifth Dimension* the axial age is described as a period of intense revelatory activity, but the locus of revelation is the human subject herself, not an active divine Being:

> Such immensely powerful moments of God-consciousness, or of Transcendence-consciousness, are what we mean by revelation. These primary revelations were so overwhelming that the lives and words of the founders communicated the reality of the Divine or the Transcendent to others, setting in motion major new currents within the stream of human religious experience.[18]

This description gives no indication of a divine activity behind revelation, only of a growing awareness on the part of human subjects of something beyond them. This pivotal period of human history suggests the kind of epoch of new awareness characteristic of Dulles's fifth model of revelation. However, while

---

[17] Hick, *Interpretation*, 12, 21–33.
[18] Hick, *The Fifth Dimension*, 78.

Hick's continued employment of the word might suggest evidence for his use of the fifth model of revelation, we can now see that such a conclusion would be mistaken. Despite occasional reference that Hick continues to make to God's revealing activity, we can identify five reasons why Hick's philosophy of religion has no place for revelation at all. Dulles' and Hick's own claims notwithstanding, Hick has developed a theology without revelation. That the idea of a non-revelatory theology may seem to be a contradiction in terms is a point to which we shall return.

The epistemic impossibility of revelation

In considering Hick's debt to Kant's epistemology we have noted the problems that attend the sharp distinction between the noumenon and its phenomenal manifestations. One important difficulty that we have seen from Kant's desire for consistency is that the noumenon can have no causal relationship to the phenomena: it is not acceptable to smuggle causality in with terms like 'influence' or 'revelation'. Admittedly, it is hard to avoid such language when interpreting Kant's work. Even in defence of Kant, Nicholas Rescher is hard pushed to avoid such language: 'it is clear that although things-in-themselves somehow "affect" the sensibility . . . the relationship here at issue is definitely not to be construed in properly causal terms'.[19] The fact is that causality is itself a category of the understanding and not something that can be applied to the thing-in-itself. Using words like 'affect' or 'influence' does not diminish this problem. All that one can do is to claim that there is a formal connection between noumenon and phenomena that we must postulate as a necessary way of explaining the existence of phenomena. This is Rescher's conclusion regarding noumenal causality in Kant's epistemology:

> Kantian noumenal causality is not actual causality at all, in the strict sense in which causality is governed by the specific, experientially constituitive Principle of Causality of the Second Analogy. Rather, it is only analogical causality, governed by a generic and regulative

---

[19] Rescher, *Kant and the Reach of Reason*, 26.

principle of grounding, a Principle of Sufficient Reason, a principle that controls what we must think to be the case, rather than what we claim to know regarding nature.[20]

This conclusion may help clarify the distinction in Kant's own work by affirming a formal connection between noumenon and phenomenon. However, this formal connection does not provide a basis for any new knowledge beyond that given in appearances. Normally, when considering Kant, critics describe this problem in terms of the inability of the human mind to penetrate beyond appearances to know the thing-in-itself, but, significantly for theology, the problem is symmetrical. It is also impossible for the thing-in-itself to reveal itself as phenomenon or as the thing-for-others. The barrier is insurmountable from either side because this epistemology supposes that all knowledge is conditioned by the mind. Therefore, there is never knowledge of the noumenon, only of phenomena. The object of all knowledge is appearance, never reality.

Responses to such a dilemma have had to claim that the barrier is not insurmountable. So just as philosophical realism presupposes that at least some aspects of reality are accessible to the human mind, the doctrine of revelation presupposes that at least some significant qualities of God may be made known to the human mind. Both philosophical realism and a doctrine of revelation assume some kind of relationship between the knower and what is known. However, in this context the very notion of relationship is problematic. A word like 'relationship' also implies cause or influence and such concepts belong to the world of appearances, not to the ultimate reality. The price of Hick's use of this Kantian insight is the impossibility of the Ultimate Real being able to disclose itself in any way, whether through inner experience or verbal prophecy. Revelation is impossible not only because direct knowledge of divine Reality is impossible; it is also impossible because the Ultimate Real cannot, in any way that we can know or describe, influence or affect the world of appearances.

---

[20] Rescher, *Kant*, 34.

The non-personal deity

In order to sustain his pluralist proposal, Hick must be able to maintain that the Ultimate Real is beyond the categories of the mind. This is an echo of Kant's conviction that the noumenon could not be conceptualised in terms of his categories of the mind. Driven by his desire to avoid privileging any one tradition over others, Hick strenuously avoids granting special place to any specific claim about what God is like. The categories of the religious mind would include concepts of the deity being either personal or non-personal. An example of a personal category is God as Father, while as non-personal one might think of the description of ultimate existence as Nirvana. Hick notes what he calls the widespread 'personification' of the Real in religions both of Semitic origin and in those identified by the west as Hindu.[21] However, to be personal is, in essence, to be in personal relationship with other centres of consciousness. While the phenomenal manifestations of the Real may be described as personal, such a quality cannot be understood to apply to the Real-in-itself: 'It follows from this that the Real *an sich* cannot be said to be personal. For this would presuppose that the Real is eternally in relation to other persons.'[22] Personality and relationship are categories belonging to human beings and therefore belong necessarily and exclusively to the order of the phenomenon. The reason why the Real is so often conceived in personal terms is, according to Hick, because knowledge is always subject to the way the knowing subject thinks. Naturally, human beings see things in personal terms. We might think how often people empathise with animal pain and assume that animal life shares a similar personal nature to ourselves. Some people even extend this empathy to plants and trees. This may seem a plausible explanation for the widespread ascription of personality to the divine being.

But this conclusion makes it difficult to understand why the Real can also be described in impersonal or non-personal terms. Hick has to be able to extend his analysis to include this apparently rival point of view and, in doing so, creates a serious difficulty for any concept of revelation. The prime example of the impersonae of the Real is

---

[21] Hick, *Interpretation*, 252–3.
[22] Hick, *Interpretation*, 264.

the Buddhist goal of Nirvana, which Hick describes as 'the Real experienced in an ineffable egolessness' in which personal identity is extinguished.[23] Other examples include Brahman and Sunyata. Hick denies that such an impersonal reality is a closer approximation to his idea of the Ultimate Real than the images of theism. He recognises that his work might suggest such a conclusion, for he admits that, to a point, 'our pluralistic hypothesis runs parallel to this central strand of Mahayana Buddhism'.[24] Indeed, one might think that there are many reasons why Hick might be tempted to ditch the pluralist hypothesis in favour of Mahayana Buddhism. However, there is one feature of this school of Buddhism that is not compatible with his philosophical pluralism. Mahayana Buddhism identifies its impersonae with the Real-in-itself, claiming that this knowledge of the Real is directly accessible through a form of mystical experience. Other images of the Real are accorded only the status of representation. Hick wants to maintain that the Real transcends both personae and impersonae such that all manifestations are only representational. Therefore, he maintains that impersonal images, like Nirvana, remain phenomenal manifestations of the noumenal real. Though the phenomenon appears in varied and even contradictory forms, each is understood to be a representation of the same reality behind them all. Pluralism accords no religion with superior epistemic status, and this means that no manifestations of the Real can be used to argue against the validity of apparently rival manifestations.

Thus far, Hick's proposal has all the hallmarks of thoroughly benign, tolerant democracy – each phenomenal manifestation has relative validity with respect to the others. The Real is neither personal nor impersonal, but such images are useful and essential in order for us to have any experience of the Real. However, this proposal is not as straightforward as it seems, for the negative demands Hick makes rule out the ultimate validity of any specific descriptions of the Real. He must then deny the personal attributes accredited to God by Christians. The qualities of love, will, faithfulness and relationship are not compatible with the attributes of Brahman or Nirvana, and so must be denied any ultimate validity.

[23] Hick, *Interpretation*, 287.

[24] Hick, *Interpretation*, 292.

They function as myths or metaphors and not as literal truth claims. Hick also tries to avoid affirming the superior validity of the impersonae of the Real over the personae by using the term 'non-personal' in contrast to impersonal images. This term is supposed to avoid giving priority either to personal or to impersonal language. After all, both being personal and being impersonal are ways in which we describe people or things of the phenomenal order. We have no right to apply either term directly to the noumenal realm.

However, it follows from this that no personal attributes of God can belong to the thing-in-itself, as they are no more than categories of personal, human experience. Therefore, the category of 'revealer' or 'being able to reveal' cannot apply to the Real-in-itself. The idea of a revealer assumes, minimally, being capable of relationship and having the will to disclose. Furthermore, in Christian terms the category assumes even more, including the possession of such qualities as purpose, faithfulness and love. Without these personal qualities the Real-in-itself is not capable of revelation in any Christian sense. Hick's noumenon, whatever else it is, cannot be a revealer. The neo-orthodox theologians placed great emphasis on the ultimate personal status of the divine in their rejection of any concept of God that defines him as object, thing, or even as one person among many persons. God is the absolute person who chooses to reveal himself: 'He can be known as absolute Subject only through the fact that He Himself makes Himself known through His own action: He is not at our disposal as an object of knowledge. He proves Himself as Lord in the fact that He, He alone, gives the knowledge of Himself, and that man has no power at his own disposal to enable him to acquire this knowledge.'[25]

This is a particularly Christian form of stating the issue: revelation is essentially the self-manifestation of the personal God who chooses to make himself known for reasons of his own. If God were not, in this sense, personal, then Christian revelation would be impossible. Furthermore, even if we were not to accept the statements of neo-orthodoxy, 'revelation' in any theistic sense must imply qualities of will and ability to communicate that are lacking in the non-personal descriptions of the noumenon. Ramachandra

---

[25] Brunner, *Revelation and Reason*, 24.

points out that it is those traditions based on the concept of historical revelation that are badly compromised by the pluralist treatment of the personal God: 'For to entertain this possibility one must then be willing to acknowledge the other possibility that this God wills to reveal God's self and enter into personal relationship with us. Hick has effectively excluded any meaningful concept of divine revelation from his "meta-religion" of religions, and so it is doubtful whether any orthodox Jew, Christian or Muslim can subscribe to it.'[26]

Cognitive freedom

I have described Hick's epistemology in terms of three steps, each of the steps in this stairway of knowledge involving increasing complexity as it relates to areas of knowledge where there is greater ambiguity. Also related to each step is an increasing cognitive freedom on the part of the believer as to how he or she may choose to interpret his or her environment. At the level of natural interpretation one may describe belief as coerced: the natural environment forces us to think and believe in a certain way. At the level of religious faith, however, interpretation is uncoerced, because this dimension is thoroughly ambiguous, permitting a plurality of interpretations. As we have seen, one major reason for this ambiguity arises from the nature of the mind itself. When analysed in Kantian terms the structure of the mind limits what claims may be made for the capabilities of reason. We simply cannot make direct claims about religious reality, because the mind is unable to perceive that reality directly. However, this is not the only reason for the ambiguity of our appreciation of religious reality. Hick also maintains a set of theological or moral reasons for this ambiguity, and it is these that form the third reason for the denial that revelation is possible.

According to Hick's theodicy, human beings must learn to use their minds properly and this includes the moral demand to turn from self-centredness to Reality-centredness: 'This greater cognitive freedom at the religious level is correlated with the greater claim upon us of the aspect of reality in question.'[27] The claim that the Real

---

[26] Ramachandra, *The Recovery of Mission*, 124–5.

[27] Hick, *Interpretation*, 161.

has upon us is related to its supreme importance as the source of value and meaning in the universe. However, the Real allows us the epistemic freedom that ensures any religious response we make to the universe will be genuinely valuable and praiseworthy. If we simply held our religious beliefs for sociological or scientific reasons, then Hick would consider them of little value. In order to ensure that human beings are truly responsible for their actions in this regard the Ultimate Real must not coerce the proper response – the moral significance of our response requires that the choice we make be utterly free. The second step of Hick's epistemology, moral interpretation, also requires this freedom, but at the third step freedom should be total. The transformation of men and women from self-centredness to Reality-centredness can only have moral value if people have the basic cognitive freedom to make autonomous decisions. We have already noticed the common anthropology shared by Hick and Kant. This common anthropology requires libertarian free will as a presupposition for human responsibility. As a result, for faith to be a good moral action on the part of the human subject, it must be uncompelled.

This commitment to absolute cognitive freedom rules out the possibility of revelation. If the divine reality were to disclose anything to us, then it would in some measure compromise the freedom of our response. Furthermore, it would privilege one community or individual over all others – a conclusion abhorrent to the philosophical pluralist.

Revelation, certainly in the first four models outlined by Dulles, implies an act on the part of some kind of revealer that makes clear something otherwise hidden. Hick cannot tolerate this implication because it would compromise true cognitive freedom. Revelation would dispel, at least for its recipients, the ambiguity of the universe. In doing so, the human subject would have less freedom to choose not to believe. The greater the extent to which revelation occurs, the more akin to natural interpretation the religious level becomes. Though human categories and concepts are still being brought to bear it would really be the divine reality that compelled the final response. We have already noted that there is incoherence in this moral argument, evident in Hick's treatment of the great religious leaders.[28]

---

[28] See Chapter 4.

They had overwhelming religious experience and yet Hick considers them fine moral examples for the rest of humanity. Granting the validity of Hick's argument, the pluralist proposal rules out proper revelation to humanity on the grounds that such revelation would compromise our pure cognitive freedom. The absence of God, described by Hick as the way he hides from us, makes faith a virtue. Revelation would spoil the moral value of religious belief.

The distinction between myth and fact

As we have seen, in Hick's scheme mythological language serves only a non-literal function. It does not inform us about an objective reality, but does encourage soteriological transformation on the part of those who use the language. Its use helps orientate the life of hearers and users towards Reality-centredness. But its use does not and cannot disclose new features of reality, a function that is the exclusive domain of factual language use. However, the nature of Ultimate Reality is too great, complex and different from us to be expressed in human language. Statements that purport to be about the Ultimate Real must then be interpreted as helpful myths rather than as cognitive truth claims. The exceptions that we noted are those purely formal descriptions of the postulates of religious life: that there is an Ultimate Real and that life extends beyond death. No more than this can be expressed in factual language.

This has serious consequences for any claim that revelation has occurred. Revelation, as the disclosure of information, could take many forms including words, events, pictures or actions. However, whatever the mode of its occurrence, for it to count as a disclosure of information it must be possible to state its meaning in propositional form.[29] Yet, according to Hick, informative statements about the Real or about supernatural reality can only be either formal, logical postulates or mythological claims. Mythological claims are not really fact asserting as we have already seen. Therefore, this leaves purely formal postulates as the sum total of our knowledge about God. However, these are not the result of revelation. Hick

---

[29] Helm argues this in *The Divine Revelation*, 21–7. Goldingay presents a rather more fluid proposal and yet still affirms this point in *Models for Scripture*, 299–313.

argues that such beliefs are postulates of human experience. In this way we find that the content of all supposed revelation can be reduced to various disclosures not of the divine but about human life. We are either giving mythological form to our feelings about ultimate purpose or we are stating a formal postulate that makes sense of our feelings. Either way, there is no disclosure from any external source. Hick's distinction between myth and fact necessarily rules out the possibility of revelation. The vast bulk of religious claims to revelation are interpreted as mythological language use and therefore this language is not taken to be fact asserting. It is designed to evoke the proper attitude or response on the part of the believer, but cannot convey any objective information. The conclusion of this account of language must be that revelation is simply self-referential language; it helps its users express their way of responding to an otherwise ambiguous universe. It yields no new truths that could transcend personal experience.

A history of the universe

A final feature of Hick's philosophy utterly demolishes the possibility of revelation. His description of the history of religions, following the work of Jaspers, is nothing more than a history of the evolution of the human consciousness. This history has no place for the revelatory activity of the Real. It may be the case that a spiritual dimension can be discerned in that evolutionary process, but, if so, such a dimension results from something inherent in human awareness rather than originating in an external source.

As we have seen, the phenomenological account of religious history offered by Hick is presented in terms of three stages of awareness. Firstly, there is the pre-axial age of corporate spirituality where religion serves the social function of preserving harmony and where individual spirituality has no function, because no distinction exists between corporate and personal identity. Secondly, the axial age itself was the period of enlightenment when personal identity was discovered and human beings related themselves to a higher dimension of love and purpose. Thirdly, the post-axial age includes some retrogressive steps but, on the whole, the primary discovery of the axial age, the I–Thou relationship, is preserved and spread through the globe.

The reason why Dulles locates Hick in the fifth model of revelation is because of this aspect of his thought. Hick's history of religions is apparently a history of revelation arising from the development of human consciousness. It was the growing awareness of individuality within society that led to a new awareness of the divine Reality indwelling all of the universe and offering purpose and goodness to individuals. However, the word 'revelation' is redundant in this account. This reading of history describes the evolution of human thought punctuated by great periods of enlightenment. Nowhere in Hick's account of history is there any need to describe a divine initiative or activity engaging the human race.

Conclusion

We have now surveyed John Hick's impressive pluralist case for regarding the major world religions as varied responses to the same Ultimate Reality; and we have also extrapolated the implications of this philosophy. The implications for a Christian believer are serious indeed. Stephen Williams also argues that Hick's doctrine of revelation, whatever else it might affirm, rules out the Christian conception of God. Williams concludes:

> [Hick] denies that we may validly think of God as personal in any way resembling the tradition. It has been difficult enough for many to swallow the claim that Christians must regard belief that God is personal as an optional belief. One is dealing with a veritable camel if one is to swallow the claim that such belief is no longer optional at all and that effectively impersonal notions of the Real are nearer the mark.[30]

Furthermore, the implications for believers of any religious tradition will find parallel problems.[31] For we may conclude that the

---

[30] Williams, 'The Trinity and "Other Religions"' in Vanhoozer (ed.), *The Trinity in a Pluralistic Age*, 38.

[31] Gavin D'Costa provides a very helpful account of the way in which Radhakrishnan's neo-Hindu philosophy must be distinguished from Hick's pluralism. Though appearing similar, Radhakrishnan argues that

pluralist case assumes that no revelation in any serious sense has ever or will ever take place. Rather, a cosmic force of some ineffable kind has created a race of people (or allowed them to come to be) and then left them to grope in the dark over the significance of their existence. The world's religions may be regarded as of roughly equal validity because they are of roughly equal invalidity – they are verbal statements made in ignorance regarding a reality about which they can know nothing of significance. This is an account of religion without revelation. Of course, Hick may be correct and many may find his arguments compelling, but they should at least be aware of where his work has taken them. The philosophical pluralist has adopted a view of the universe in which God is notable only for his absence.

Pluralists have one key line of defence to any critique: they question what credible alternative there could be. In my closing chapter I shall attempt a brief answer to that question. Indeed, it will become evident that there is an alternative, which, far from closing down inter-religious encounter and understanding, might even make it more productive and fruitful.

---

[31] (*Continued*) there may be direct mystical apprehension of the Absolute and, therefore, in this sense there is still a revealed knowledge of the divine; D'Costa, *The Meeting of Religions and the Trinity*, 63.

Chapter 10

Liberty and Religious Diversity

Faith without History

In my biographical survey of Hick's career I have sought to demonstrate a certain trajectory to his work. His initial commitment to an
orthodox Christian theology established certain foundations for his
thought. However, he also held a fundamental commitment to the
philosophical tradition of the Enlightenment, which was evident in
his epistemology. Hick developed a theory of knowledge in which
Christian theology was peripheral. His central commitment was to
a largely secular philosophical position in which God's presence is
not evident, but is a matter of interpretation. Yet this is not to deny
that his philosophical work is formidable, as Hick is an effective philosopher. The point here is that the philosophical position he
develops is inevitably hostile to any form of orthodox Christianity.

It has been my claim that Hick's position has never had to
undergo a radical revolution. His life's work has been a matter of his
theology catching up with his philosophy. The religious-pluralist
account, which is a natural position for anyone who adopts the
'modernist' outlook, may well become the most popular account of
religion within the liberal tradition. Sceptical of any claim to absolute certainty regarding religious belief, the position assumes that
the most important beliefs will be those that are truths of reason,
rather than those based on historical events or people. This position
inevitably jettisons the Judaeo-Christian commitment to revelation
through history.

Hick is dependent on a philosophical position that must drasti-
cally revise the meaning of Christianity. Rather than affirming the
central significance of a historic incarnation and divine revelation,

Hick affirms only a few simple beliefs. Three core beliefs survive pluralist reinterpretation: the existence of some kind of divine reality, the possibility of continued existence beyond the grave, and the moral value of selfless behaviour. Unsurprisingly, these few beliefs are largely compatible with all the major religious traditions of the world.

From a Christian point of view, the major weakness that must be identified in Hick's account is its rejection both of historical evidence and of its significance, a weakness inherent in his epistemology. Traditional Christian theology, in contrast, would put great emphasis on the concept of God revealing himself through history. The Scriptures themselves are held to be a historical revelation of God; therefore, the Christian doctrine of the knowledge of God must at least imply knowledge through history. However, in Hick's framework, history is displaced by personal experience. In his terms, our knowledge of God is really nothing more than a reflection on our personal experience of the universe. That there is a divine reality behind this experience is an assumption made by those with religious faith. As I have sought to show throughout this work, such a weak treatment of history is derived from Hick's epistemology. While Hume had provided a powerful critique of knowledge based on observation and history, after him Kant, among other philosophers, developed a theory of knowledge and religion that did not regard truth as dependent on history. Hick's religious pluralism is a natural outcome of this Enlightenment movement.

Hick's treatment of history sidelines the significance of any events that might privilege a religion. For philosophical reasons, the truths of history cannot be seen as necessary to faith, which leads Hick to what must be described as a non-Christian view of history. His account fits better with what many would understand to be the traditions of Hindu culture, rather than those of Christianity. D'Costa identifies the crucial connection between Christianity and history: 'For the Semitic religions the events of history tend to be all important and decisive. For example, if Jesus did not die on the cross, then by implication the resurrection appearances and the events that followed would be cast in a vastly different light.'[1]

---

[1] D'Costa, *John Hick's Theology of Religions*, 106–7.

Such an implication does not trouble Hick, because he defines faith as a way of interpreting the universe rather than as a response to historic events. Therefore, all events and revelations of history are reinterpreted as mythological. However, Hick cannot avoid offering some interpretation of the significance of the historical Jesus. We have found that his interpretation is largely dismissive of the Christian tradition and sceptical of the historical sources. What little we can affirm of Jesus, Hick claims, suggests that he was a pluralist of sorts. Indeed, all that can be deduced from the historical evidence is that Jesus would have been admired by any religious culture. It just happens to be the case that Jesus was admired in the Greek culture and understood in Greek philosophical terms, but had Jesus been admired among those in the Hindu cultures then a different description would have emerged. D'Costa points out the difficulty with this reading of history: 'It is pure hypothesis that if Christianity had expanded eastwards, Jesus would have been identified as a Bodhisattva or Avatar. In fact, it is interesting to note that when Christianity did spread eastwards at a very early date, if the tradition of St Thomas' arrival in India is true, no such process occurred.'[2]

Christianity did develop in the east – and yet a low Christology did not emerge there. The fact is that a high Christology has always been part of the Christian tradition. It is impossible to get back 'behind' the historical sources to unearth a person who fits Hick's claim. Hick's reconstructed Jesus is pure conjecture, and it is not surprising that his conjecture leads to an image of a person who would support the pluralist hypothesis.

This is not to deny that Christian theology has developed in the course of the years. Yet those developments may be entirely legitimate. C.F.D. Moule has provided convincing evidence that Christology did not 'evolve' during early church history – on the contrary, he demonstrates that a high view of Christ is already embedded in the New Testament and developed, rather than evolved, in the course of later theological reflection. In particular, Christ is seen as an individual, distinct, in important respects, from his followers. According to Moule the disciples 'attribute to him a unique closeness to God and a divine, creative initiative, which

---

[2] D'Costa, *Theology of Religions*, 121.

marks him off from their conception of what each believer – precisely because of him and through him – may become'.[3]

Moule's evidence includes the divine title, LORD (Greek *kurios*), which the Greek-speaking Jews used to translate the Hebrew name for God in the Old Testament. In the New Testament the word need only identify a term of great respect, but its use in relation to Jesus is highly significant. Some New Testament passages that apply the title to Jesus do so in a way that deliberately echoes the Old Testament background (e.g. Phil. 2:6–11 seen in relation to Isa. 45:22–4). Moule also points out the way worship is offered to Jesus in the New Testament and the claims regarding his resurrection. All of this evidence belongs to the earliest strands of the New Testament, and it is these that are developed in later church tradition. It may be established that the high Christology of Scripture does not simply arise in later reflection, but is part of the very earliest witness of the New Testament. Paul Barnett has taken up this theme. He provides impressive evidence from the earliest letters of the New Testament and demonstrates that a high Christology was no later ecclesiastical development, but the very cause of the existence of the church.

> [T]he letters point to early and shared convictions of an exalted kind about Jesus. The non-evangelistic nature of the letters indicates that these convictions are shared by both writer and readers . . . The most plausible – *historically plausible* – explanation of the early and exalted view of Jesus is the percussive impact of Jesus the Teacher, risen from the dead, upon his immediate followers, both before and after Easter.[4]

In contrast, there is little evidence for the minimalist Christology of Hick, who relies on suppositions regarding what lay behind the formation of the New Testament. He dismisses the claim that a high Christology is implicit in the gospels, but he does not do so through by exegesis.[5] His rejection of an orthodox Christology tends always

---

[3] Moule, *The Origin of Christology*, 103. I discuss this point in Sinkinson, *John Hick: An Introduction to his Theology*, 28–32.

[4] Barnett, *Jesus and the Logic of History*, 56.

[5] Hick is generally approving of Moule's scholarship (along with that of James Dunn) but dismissive of their conclusions. See *The Metaphor of God Incarnate*, 28–39.

to return to his objection that the doctrine makes no sense – at least, not to Hick. His alternative doctrine of Christ is one entirely in keeping with his understanding of revelation: given that the Ultimate Real is unable to communicate in any form with the human race, it is clearly impossible that the Ultimate Real could ever take on human form. Because revelation is not possible, history is of little significance to the pluralist argument. Hick does have a great deal to say about the historical development of religious traditions, but only as he seeks to reinterpret their ideas in the light of his hypothesis. There are no specific truth claims regarding religious reality that can be gleaned from history. Even the discoveries of the axial age and the great religious founders are directly accessible to religious awareness in our own time. As those discoveries do not depend on their historical context in the axial age, Hick's epistemology emphasises present experience, not past events.

It is important to press the point that Hick's theological commitments are seriously compromised by this philosophical scepticism. Christian thought has developed on the basis of a historical revelation of God in Christ. Notice the way in which Hick rejects the arguments of exclusivists:

> But can it possibly be the will of the loving heavenly Father of Jesus' teaching that only that minority of men and women who have the luck to be born into a Christian part of the world can enter eternal life? This would not be the work of a God of limitless and universal love, who values all human beings equally, but an arbitrary cosmic tyrant.[6]

Hick offers an important and serious objection, which requires careful thought and response. In recent decades many orthodox Christian theologians have tried to deal with just such an objection.[7] However, the reason for noticing the objection here is to question whether Hick has the right to raise it. Why should the Ultimate Real be a God of universal love rather than a cosmic tyrant? Why

---

[6] Hick, 'Response to R. Douglas Geivett and W. Gary Phillips' in Ockholm and Phillips (eds.), *Four Views on Salvation in a Pluralistic World*, 250.

[7] From an evangelical point of view this would include, among many others, the contributors to Sanders (ed.), *What about Those who Have Never Heard?*; and Anderson, *Christianity and World Religions*.

should the Ultimate Real be a loving heavenly Father rather than an impersonal absolute? Without a high Christology, Hick's objection lacks weight. Writing before *An Interpretation of Religion* was published, critics already noted the difficulty into which Hick was putting himself. Gillis, for example, commented, 'Hick's conception of theocentrism is based upon his understanding of God, and his understanding of God is a particular one which derives from the manifestation of God in Christ.'[8]

The original impetus for the pluralist hypothesis lay with Hick's conception of an impartial and all-loving God, a concept Christian theology derives from Christology. If Jesus Christ is himself the supreme revelation of God then we are able to speak in personal terms of the character and values of God. Describing God as love, the apostle John writes, 'God's love was revealed among us in this way: God sent his only Son into the world so that we might live through him. In this is love, not that we loved God but that he loved us and sent his Son to be the atoning sacrifice for our sins' (1 John 4:9-10). Hick's weaker 'theocentrism' would make this difficult to sustain. Without a high Christology the Christian understanding of the love of God is under question. Worse still, without a concept of God as personal the very notion of a loving God is rendered meaningless. Also commenting before *An Interpretation of Religion*, D'Costa writes, 'I believe that Hick severs the ground from under his Copernican feet. This is so because in arguing for the Copernican revolution on the premise of a God of universal love, such a position entails precisely that one form of revelation of God is definitive and normative compared to others.'[9]

The very ground upon which Hick states his pluralist hypothesis was compromised by his low Christology and dismissal of historical revelation. However, with the publication of his more recent major work this objection becomes fatal. As we have seen the very possibility of revelation is rendered impossible in his later statement of the pluralist hypothesis; and without revelation there is nothing we can say about the Ultimate Real with any conviction.

We have traced Hick's epistemology from its development as part of a Christian worldview to its use in the pluralist hypothesis.

---

[8] Gillis, *A Question of Final Belief*, 171.
[9] D'Costa, *Theology of Religions*, 102.

While his epistemology has not undergone radical revision, the attendant theology has changed out of all recognition. My argument has been that this is because his epistemology is devoid of the possibility of revelation. Without a God who reveals, there is nothing significant that can be said about the Ultimate Real. History is of marginal significance. Whatever claims are made about history – an exodus from Egypt or a physical resurrection of a Messiah – are reduced to vague possibilities. The truths of history are uncertain – only the truths of reason demand absolute loyalty. The consequence of this is a minimalist theology: Hick offers to the world religions an emaciated 'god' that is neither personal nor non-personal, neither good nor evil, neither existing nor non-existing. This 'god' reveals nothing, never intervenes and is inaccessible to prayer. Such a 'god' is compatible with all because it is without definition.

Inter-Religious Encounter

Hick's position is attractive for a number of reasons, and his work will obviously appeal to those who are already committed to some form of post-Kantian epistemology. However, there is also great appeal to traditional Christians. This appeal owes much to the possibilities pluralism offers for inter-religious co-operation, for pluralists would claim that their way of thinking engenders humility and respect for those of other faiths.

Christians find a strong moral force in the argument that one should approach others in humility with the expectation that we might learn from them.[10] However, for Hick this is more than a matter of attitude. Religious pluralism is founded upon an 'epistemic' humility. In other words, built into his theory of knowledge is scepticism regarding the validity of religious truth claims. We have seen how Hick outlines three levels of knowledge, each offering an increasing level of ambiguity, ignorance and

---

[10] Among evangelicals this has led to much creativity and debate. These varied positions are surveyed in Sanders, *No Other Name*. Clark Pinnock has been at the forefront of this debate and evangelical interaction with his position on the world religions is to be found in Gray and Sinkinson (eds.), *Reconstructing Theology*, 155–265.

uncertainty. This is related to an increasing sense of humility on the part of the knower. For example, in matters of scientific debate or common sense – such as our claim that the earth revolves around the sun during the course of the year – Hick could argue that there is little need for epistemic humility. Of course, our attitude should always remain humble, but we are permitted a sense of absolute conviction regarding this belief, a belief on the first step of knowledge.

The second step concerns moral belief. There are some moral beliefs about which we need have no humility, because they are so universally acknowledged. The evils of murder and rape along with greed, pride and arrogance are matters we can hold to as absolutely wrong. However, there are many further moral issues that are much less certain. Hick might suggest issues of sexual fidelity, abortion or euthanasia as areas about which we must humbly acknowledge uncertainty. Indeed, Hick describes euthanasia as an ethical possibility which cannot be settled absolutely. It is a matter of relative, personal choice: 'each individual, rather than the state or the medical profession, should – in my opinion – have the right to make the final decision in this area'.[11] Related to this level of interpretation is our aesthetic response to reality. While it is still possible to speak of broad agreement over what is beautiful or ugly there remains great freedom over such subjective evaluations.

However, in matters of religious belief we arrive at the third step of knowledge. The need for humility is most important here. According to Hick, we must not make absolute claims or hold with unshakable conviction matters of religious concern. When we are discussing our religious beliefs in philosophical terms, we must admit that our beliefs have shaky foundations and are highly likely to be, at best, only partially true.

The kind of humility Hick commends leads to a certain kind of inter-religious dialogue. If all the dialogue partners share this epistemology then they will all be able to suspend their personal convictions and admit that what they believe is open to doubt. Religious pluralism is an attractive framework for those interested in inter-religious co-operation. Rather than being divided by contrary doctrines, believers might find unity in a common ethical agenda.

---

[11] Hick, *The Fifth Dimension*, 252.

A good example of such an agenda is to be found in the 1993 Declaration of the Parliament of the World's Religions. This was a major international assembly of representatives from many religious groupings of the world. Its purpose was to agree upon and commend to the world a statement of common ethical values. The declaration is a broad statement of ecological concern, the importance of community, the need to treat others as we would be treated, and a rejection of greed and injustice. The declaration does not mention God and avoids any specific language that might be taken to exclude certain religious groups. Hans Küng wrote, 'The hope is that this document may set off a process which changes the behaviour of men and women in the religions in the direction of understanding, respect and cooperation.'[12] Concerns over the nature of God were excluded from the development at the outset.[13] Indeed, Küng freely acknowledged that 'a consensus can be achieved in matters relating to a global ethic only if . . . one leaves aside all differences of faith and 'dogma', symbols and rites, and concentrates on common guidelines for human conduct'.[14]

While Küng has argued against Hick's form of pluralism, there is no doubt that theological pluralism encourages exactly this kind of attitude to creeds and rites. Moreover, pluralism provides theoretical justification for the strategy of Küng, who sounds like a pragmatist in his commitment to finding a global ethic. The specific content of religious belief *must* be laid aside in favour of vague, common criteria because only when this is done will cooperation be truly possible. Hick's position offers philosophical reasons to lay aside such specific beliefs. The 'Global Ethic' declaration is a good example of the kind of agenda that inevitably takes centre stage when religious pluralism is adopted. Matters of doctrinal difference or contrasting worship practices are laid aside as somewhat extraneous in favour of this allegedly neutral agenda. One can easily see how Hick's pluralist hypothesis provides a very ready and attractive theoretical basis for the kind of work the Parliament of the World Religions is engaged in.

---

[12] Küng and Kuschel, *A Global Ethic*, 8.
[13] Küng and Kuschel, *Ethic*, 61.
[14] Küng and Kuschel, *Ethic*, 65.

These seem to be great strengths in the religious pluralist position particularly as it relates to the encounter of different religions. For a Christian there is the obvious humility it seems to engender along with respect for others and a basis for co-operation. However, we may now identify problems with this strategy. The virtues of humility and tolerance entailed by the pluralist hypothesis are more apparent than real. It is this fact that shows the deepest weakness of religious pluralism. Far from being a philosophy of tolerance, it leads to a serious form of intellectual intolerance.

Humility and Tolerance

Humility is a virtue (Gal. 5:23; Eph. 4:2; 1 Pet. 3:8). The English word finds its etymological roots in the Latin word for lowly or earthly. The New Testament word (*prautēs*), 'refers to a trait of character independent of any conditions of poverty . . . political powerlessness or oppression'.[15] A great example of humility is given to us in the gospel account of Jesus washing the feet of his disciples. By this action he gave an example of his role as a servant of others. The Christian church has only really been true to its master when it too has been a servant of others. Even the proper growth of the church has come through humble service rather than violent oppression or mastery. Humility implies that one freely lays aside rights or privileges in order to put others first and serve them. In no sense does the humility of Jesus imply that he lacked knowledge or insight; it is exactly because of his high degree of knowledge and power that Christ is considered such a matchless example of humility. In contrast, Hick's account only appears to commend humility. There is no reason why religious believers may not have absolute convictions regarding the truth of their beliefs and yet exercise profound humility. Thus one must find fault with the kind of claim made by the pluralist Wilfred Cantwell Smith. Regarding the statement 'Without the particular knowledge of God in Jesus Christ, men do not really know God at all' he writes, 'Let us leave aside for the moment any question of whether or not this is true . . . My point

---

[15] Reid, 'Humility' in Atkinson and Field (eds.), *New Dictionary of Christian Ethics and Pastoral Theology*, 470.

here is simply that, in any case, it is arrogant. At least it becomes arrogant when one carries it out to the non-Western or non-Christian world.'[16]

Smith's point is either trivial or false. If he simply means that making an absolute truth claim is necessarily arrogant then that is a trivial point. It would be equally arrogant to say, 'Without knowledge of the Copernican system, people do not really understand the motion of the planets at all.' There is a trivial sense in which all truth claims are arrogant. However, if Smith means that whenever the claim is made it always implies a morally abhorrent attitude then his point is false. Lesslie Newbigin defends an orthodox doctrine of the incarnation, but denies the charge of arrogance. 'No human mind can grasp the depth of that mystery. But, having been laid hold of by it, no human being can think of it as merely one among many symbols of an unknowable reality. To affirm that this is truth, not merely truth for me but truth for all, is not arrogance. It is simply responsible human behaviour.'[17]

Furthermore, Hick's form of religious pluralism is built upon its own absolutes. It is not true to claim that religious pluralism means laying aside all personal convictions and treating one's own knowledge as provisional. Hick's pluralism only requires we do this with regard to our distinctive religious beliefs. There are a number of other beliefs to which we must hold absolute allegiance. Primarily these beliefs are those entailed by the golden rule to love others as we would be loved. This moral ethic, isolated from any specific religious context, looks remarkably similar to a modern liberal agenda. Hick sees no need for humility regarding this ethical agenda. The underlying incoherence of the religious pluralist project is that it requires intellectual humility regarding all religious positions other than its own. Hick would claim that religious pluralism is exempt from this requirement because it is not itself a religion. This, however, may only be a case of special pleading and reveals a blind spot in the pluralist argument. Even if 'pluralism' is not, in itself, a religion, it so reframes the religion of the pluralist that it becomes a new form of religion. The religion of a 'Christian pluralist' is quite

---

[16] Smith, *Patterns of Faith Around the World*, 135.
[17] Newbigin, 'Religion for the Marketplace' in D'Costa (ed.), *Christian Uniqueness Reconsidered*, 138–9.

different from the religion of an 'evangelical Christian'. To this religion of 'Christian pluralism' there is absolute loyalty.

It would be better to refrain from applying humility to epistemology. Humility is a virtue and, as a character trait, to be cultivated throughout life. The way that we speak to others of our beliefs will be shaped by the trait of humility. However, the convictions with which we hold to our beliefs and the manner in which we commend them to others are distinct issues. The religious pluralist position is a case in point. Hick's form of pluralism offers a clear structure of belief including absolute claims regarding what we cannot know and absolute moral demands. However, whether the religious pluralist is a humble person or not is a separate issue. Someone might be absolutely certain of something they know and yet communicate that knowledge with great humility.

Destroying Diversity

We may press this point regarding tolerance further and ask whether religious pluralism really produces tolerance at all. Hick rejects exclusivism and inclusivism for being intolerant. Both positions, it is supposed, make assumptions about others regarding the validity of their beliefs. However, Hick cannot avoid making such assumptions either. Indeed, the philosophy of language embedded in the pluralist hypothesis demands a constant reinterpretation of the claims religious people make. The pluralist interprets the doctrines of all traditions as, substantially, mythological. The only religious claims that escape the mythological treatment are those that the pluralist herself makes. This leads D'Costa to a devastating exposition of Hick's implicit exclusivism. Describing Hick's treatment of all religious truth claims as mythological (other than those made by the pluralist), he writes, 'As I have shown, such a position has the effect of claiming that there are no true religions, for all misunderstand themselves until they embrace the pluralist hypothesis. They must fundamentally reinterpret their self-understanding in modernity's terms.'[18]

---

[18] D'Costa, *The Meeting of Religions and the Trinity*, 46.

The pluralist hypothesis cannot tolerate division or dissent; it must always reinterpret the claims others make in order to fit its own conclusions. In a sense, Hick could claim this is true of any hypothesis.[19] It is unavoidable that one will depart from the self-understanding of those one interprets. But at least the traditional Christian exclusivist is explicit about this. The pluralist position is reticent about its underlying exclusivism. Furthermore, the exclusivist interpretation of religions allows symbols and scriptures to speak for themselves even if this highlights divergence.[20] The pluralist interpretation allows no such disparity. Moreover, it is not even clear how a pluralist could ever recognise a contradiction. We have seen how even the most contrary claims – regarding the existence of God or the crucifixion of Jesus – may be construed as compatible when subjected to mythological interpretation. As long as religious people bear moral fruits the pluralist hypothesis exorcises any remaining divisions from among them. However things may appear, good religious people simply cannot be in real disagreement over matters of ultimate religious significance.

One assumption running through much pluralist rhetoric is that division and disagreement is a bad thing. The orthodox doctrine of the incarnation and its attendant missionary impetus are rejected, among other reasons, for encouraging disagreement among religious people. For example, consider again the argument of Smith: 'Any position that antagonizes and alienates rather than reconciles, that is arrogant rather than humble, that promotes segregation rather than fellowship, that is unlovely, is *ipso facto* un-Christian.'[21] Rather like Hick, Smith continues to use his Christian assumptions to justify his pluralist case. However, his argument here relies upon the ambiguity of his language. Antagonism, arrogance and segregation would all be un-Christian in matters of personal relationships, justice and racial equality. But Smith applies these attitudes to cover truth itself. His argument is mistaken because truth-claiming necessarily causes 'segregation'. Truth must be segregated from error.

---

[19] Hick does so in 'The Possibility of Religious Pluralism: A Reply to Gavin D'Costa', 161–6.

[20] This point is taken up against Smith in Sinkinson, 'Scripture and scriptures: The Problem of Hermeneutics in Inter-religious Understanding'.

[21] Smith, *Patterns*, 135.

Christian faith can be distinguished from non-Christian doctrines and beliefs; and this need not imply racism or any other form of immoral behaviour.

The pluralist approach to religions is far from tolerant. It assumes the supremacy of the post-Kantian, liberal outlook and interprets all religions from this vantage point. Hick denies the charge that he interprets religions from a neutral position. He does this by pointing out that he arrives at his position 'inductively', starting with his own Christian experience.[22] This response is beside the point. His personal position may have started out with his own experience within the Christian community, but it has inductively led him to an intellectual hypothesis that claims no particular religious affiliation. As a matter of fact, it is affiliated to the post-Kantian worldview with its hallmarks of secularism. Some pluralists have been more strident in their admission of this point. For example, one educator influenced by the pluralist case concedes, 'Pluralism and secularism are two sides of the same coin; education for pluralism means education for secularism.'[23] Far from providing a framework in which diverse religions can coexist in tolerance, respect *and* disagreement, the pluralist hypothesis subjects every religion to this secular agenda. Religious diversity appears to be valued when pluralists engage in dialogue, but on their fundamental commitments they are in agreement. Pluralists, whatever their religious background, differ only over what, to them, are secondary matters of marginal importance. Pluralism ultimately leads us to secularism where religions are tolerated only insofar as they make no absolute claims and cause no trouble. The specific, distinct claims of historical revelation are jettisoned.

Christians and Tolerance

The pluralist emphasis on tolerance may appear attractive in comparison with even a brief survey of church history. Its critics often highlight the repression and ugly intolerance apparent in the

---

[22] Hick, *The Rainbow of Faiths*, 50.
[23] Narchison, 'Theological Education for Pluralism in India' in May (ed.), *Pluralism and the Religions*, 67.

church. Sadly, many would grant that Bertrand Russell has a point when he boldly declares, 'At all times, from the age of Constantine to the end of the seventeenth century, Christians were far more fiercely persecuted by other Christians than they ever were by the Roman emperors.'[24] But it is important to question why such intolerance should have emerged. I would deny that it arose from an exclusive loyalty to Jesus Christ as Lord. Given the moral demands and example of the Jesus of the gospels it seems untenable to claim that devotion to him would inspire such behaviour. I shall briefly claim here that a mistaken view of diversity developed in the early Constantinian period of the church. This leads to an ironic conclusion: far from dealing with this mistake, the religious pluralist strategy prolongs it.

Since the time of Constantine, many Christians have tended to believe in a territorial church. This is evident in the concept of 'Christendom'. This concept assumes that everyone living in a region will subscribe to the same creed and church structures. For much of the history of the Christian church there has been a willingness to use physical or legal coercion in order to conform society to one, shared belief system. Michael Grant describes Constantine's outlook in these terms:

> Constantine wanted an established church, to which all good Christians would belong; and those who would not belong to it were dismissed as 'heretics' – a term resounding with mutual Christian accusations, and with a long and ominous history ahead of it. Constantine deplored this ridiculous proliferation of dissension, believing that imperial unity required unity of creeds.[25]

Social harmony and unity was assumed to require a doctrinal harmony. It is this commitment to a unified church and state that seems to be the key motivation to crush diversity. Heresy and sectarianism were identified as the same thing. Leonard Verduin notes that the etymological roots of 'heretic' are a verb that means, 'to exercise option in the presence of alternatives'. This gave rise to the idea that 'Those who saw the Christian life to be a matter of choice between

---

[24] Russell, *Why I Am Not a Christian*, 35.
[25] Grant, *The Emperor Constantine*, 162.

alternatives were for that reason called "heretics" by those who thought in terms of a "choiceless Christianity".[26] Of course, while these controversies raged over diversity within the Christian church, the principles apply more generally. Those who saw the Christian life as a path chosen rather than imposed would have to acknowledge that there are a plurality of choices. It is not that all paths would be equally valid or lead to the same destination, but that it is valid for society to tolerate a plurality of options. Nonetheless, to describe faith in these terms was rejected as heresy.

Any group that refused to accept the ecclesiastical structures of Christendom were identified as heretics, even though they may have believed most of the same fundamental doctrines as the rest of the church. This was true in the treatment of the Donatists[27] and later of the Anabaptists.[28] Christendom had little concept of religious freedom and diversity. Nonetheless, not all Christians have been captive to the assumptions of Christendom. As an example we might consider the Anabaptist movement.

The Anabaptists earned their nickname from their practice of only baptising believers and, therefore, rebaptising those who had been baptised as children. But this practice was only one way their understanding of the relationship between church and state was expressed. Central to their understanding was belief in a gathered church. They held that the church is a gathering together of those who believe in Jesus Christ. The state is a wider body of people who may only belong to the church through personal profession of faith; in this, the Anabaptists, who were able to distinguish between the roles of church and state, dissented from the prevailing view of Christendom. However, the contrary idea of Christendom was

---

[26] Verduin, *The Reformers and their Stepchildren*, 72.

[27] Of whom Willis says that 'they were for the most part orthodox in doctrine, though schismatical in practice'; *Saint Augustine and the Donatist Controversy*, 129–30.

[28] There is not space here to discuss the various assessments of the Donatists and Anabaptists. No doubt, various theological, ethical and political views are covered by these terms. Nonetheless, in such movements one detects early forms of nonconformist thought and in responding to pluralism they offer fresh insights. The way that these dissenting voices were treated by Christendom is particularly instructive. On the Donatists see Grant, *The Emperor Constantine*, 164–7.

unfortunately carried over into much of the church of the Reformation. For example, Douglas Kelly notes that John Calvin 'has no concept of a separation between religion and state, or of non-Christian magistrate, or of toleration of plural churches'.[29] Because both state and church were held to be accountable to a transcendent law, continuing public persecution of heresy and sectarian worship was permitted, and both church and magistrate condemned false doctrine. So ingrained in the church was this attitude that one minister was deposed in Strasbourg for claiming 'that the magistrate must leave every man to his own devices in regard to religion, no matter what he believes or teaches, so long as he does not disturb the outward civil quiet'.[30]

That such convictions should be denounced as heresy demonstrates how ingrained the notion of Christendom, with its intolerance of diversity, had become even among Christians of the Reformation: those who had been persecuted under the late mediaeval church themselves became persecutors almost overnight. Many Reformers failed to grasp that the promotion of freedom of conscience in matters of religious belief was compatible with evangelical orthodoxy. The dissenting voice of the Anabaptist movement offered an alternative.[31]

There was fierce and violent opposition to the Baptist distinction between belonging to the church and belonging to the state. It was claimed that to make such a distinction was political nihilism and showed no respect for proper government. Verduin notes that such charges were only possible because of 'the (mistaken) notion that society cannot hang together unless it is bound together in a common religion'.[32] Baptists were rediscovering a proper Christian distinction between belonging together in some form of society and belonging to the church. Of course, it is not only Baptists who have affirmed this distinction and nor do all Baptists consistently adhere to it. Nonetheless, the distinction gains credibility now that the

---

[29] Kelly, *The Emergence of Liberty in the Modern World*, 26.

[30] Verduin, *Reformers*, 46.

[31] There is not space here to develop this point in detail but the reader is directed to the important work of Nigel Goring Wright in *Discovering Constantine*.

[32] Verduin, *Reformers*, 104.

western world has dropped its claim to be a Christian society. Christians living in the post-Christian west must find ways of remaining loyal to Christ while affirming social tolerance of non-Christians. There is much to learn in this from the legacy of the dissenting churches. A Christian theology of religions needs to be able to recognise differences and permit diversity.

It is an irony that in their response to religious diversity, pluralists are the ones in danger of committing the mistake of Christendom. They argue that the diversity of religions must be explained by some common core experience or overarching ethical project. If we are to live in harmony as a society the pluralist assumes we must also share a harmony of creed. Consequently, a philosopher like Hick is driven to develop a neutral, philosophical interpretation that can explain away religious differences. Religious pluralism is intellectual intolerance – it cannot tolerate the possibility that other religions might be genuinely 'other', but seeks to reinterpret them, even against their practitioners' wishes. Pluralists remove the grounds of disagreement, particularly historical revelation, and in doing so think they have struck a victory for toleration – but it is a Pyrrhic victory. The price of the pluralist hypothesis is the ultimate validity of the things that distinguish religions and give them their uniqueness. The world religions are reduced to the bland and insipid values of secular modernity with all its attendant inability to answer great questions. As MacIntyre points out in his critique of modernity, 'The facts of disagreement themselves frequently go unacknowledged, disguised by a rhetoric of consensus.'[33]

Conclusion

Hick often argues that his position is the 'best' hypothesis. He is willing to concede that he may be wrong, but challenges anyone who would say so to provide something better. On the face of it this is a very honest challenge, but the problem with it lies in specifying what 'best' might mean. The 'best' hypothesis for Hick is clearly the one that reconciles conflicting religions and removes the need for argument. The 'best' hypothesis for the pluralist will always adhere

---

[33] MacIntyre, *Whose Justice? Which Rationality?*, 2.

to the principles of modern liberalism with its treatment of history and equality. However, the 'best' hypothesis could be defined differently. The 'best' might be one that allows a Christian humbly to contradict major doctrinal commitments of other religions and still live at peace with them. This is why mission is a perfectly valid response to religious diversity. Christian mission is not a matter of coercion or imposition. Mission is the peaceful offer of good news to societies and individuals who are given the freedom, as creatures made in the image of God, to reject that offer. What my analysis has shown is that the tolerance encouraged by religious pluralism requires a primary commitment to a shared worldview in which personal experience is coterminous with 'god' and where that 'god' can reveal nothing. Far from being the 'best' hypothesis to interpret the world religions, it is a hypothesis that represents their death warrant.

Bibliography

Allen, Charlotte, *The Human Christ* (Oxford: Lion, 1998)

Allen, Diogenes, *Christian Belief in a Postmodern World* (Louisville: Westminster/John Knox, 1989)

Anderson, Norman, *Christianity and World Religions* (Leicester: IVP, 1984)

Atkinson, David J., and David H. Field (eds.), *New Dictionary of Christian Ethics and Pastoral Theology* (Leicester: IVP, 1995)

Ayer, A.J., *Language, Truth and Logic* (London: Victor Gollancz, 1946)

Badham, Paul (ed.), *A John Hick Reader* (London: Macmillan, 1990)

—, 'John Hick's *An Interpretation of Religion*' in Harold Hewitt (ed.), *Problems in the Philosophy of Religion* (London: Macmillan, 1991)

Barbour, Ian G., *Myths, Models and Paradigms* (London: SCM, 1974)

Barnes, Philip L., 'Continuity and Development in John Hick's Theology', *Studies in Religion* 21/4 (1992), 395–402

Barnett, Paul W., *Jesus and the Logic of History* (Leicester: Apollos, 1997)

Bettenson, Henry, *Documents of the Christian Church* (Oxford: OUP, 1967)

Brunner, Emil, *Revelation and Reason* (London: SCM, 1947)

Byrne, Peter, 'John Hick's Philosophy of World Religions', *Scottish Journal of Theology* 35 (1982), 298–301

Calvin, John, *Institutes of the Christian Religion*, 2 vols. (tr. J. Beveridge; London: James Clarke, 1949)

Carson, D.A., *The Gagging of God* (Leicester: IVP, 1996)

Cook, Robert, 'Postmodernism, Pluralism and John Hick', *Themelios* 19/1 (1993), 10–11

D'Costa, Gavin, *John Hick's Theology of Religions* (Lanham: University Press of America, 1987)

—, 'John Hick and Religious Pluralism: Yet Another Revolution' in Harold Hewitt (ed.), *Problems in the Philosophy of Religion* (London: Macmillan, 1991)

—, *The Meeting of Religions and the Trinity* (Edinburgh: T. & T. Clark, 2000)

D'Costa, Gavin (ed.), *Christian Uniqueness Reconsidered* (New York: Orbis, 1990)

DiNoia, J.A., 'Varieties of Religious Aims: Beyond Exclusivism, Inclusivism, and Pluralism' in Bruce Marshall (ed.), *Theology and Dialogue* (Notre Dame: University of Notre Dame Press, 1990)

Dulles, Avery, *Models of Revelation* (London: Gill & Macmillan, 1992)

Eddy, Paul R., 'John Hick's Theological Pilgrimage' in *Proceedings of the Wheaton Theology Conference* (Illinois: Wheaton College, 1992)

—, 'Religious Pluralism and the Divine: Another Look at John Hick's Neo-Kantian Proposal', *Religious Studies* 30 (1994), 467–78

Ferguson, Sinclair B., and David F. Wright (eds.), *New Dictionary of Theology* (Leicester: IVP, 1989)

Forrester, D.B., 'Professor Hick and the Universe of Faiths', *Scottish Journal of Theology* 29 (1976), 65–72

Gellner, Ernest, *Reason and Culture* (Oxford: Blackwell, 1992)

Gillis, Chester, *A Question of Final Belief* (London: Macmillan, 1989)

Godlove, Terry F., *Religion, Interpretation, and Diversity of Belief* (Cambridge: CUP, 1989)

Goldingay, John, *Models For Scripture* (Carlisle: Paternoster, 1994)

Grant, Michael, *The Emperor Constantine* (London: Phoenix Giant, 1993)

Gray, Tony, and Christopher Sinkinson (eds.), *Reconstructing Theology* (Carlisle: Paternoster, 2000)

Grenz, Stanley J., and Roger E. Olson, *20th Century Theology* (Carlisle: Paternoster, 1992)

Hawkes, Terence, *Metaphor* (London: Methuen, 1984)

Helm, Paul, *The Varieties of Belief* (London: George Allen & Unwin, 1973)

—, *The Divine Revelation* (London: Marshall, Morgan & Scott, 1982)

—, *Belief Policies* (Cambridge: CUP, 1994)

Hick, John, 'The Christology of D.M. Baillie', *Scottish Journal of Theology* 11 (1958), 1–12

—, *Arguments for the Existence of God* (London: Macmillan, 1970)

—, *Death and Eternal Life* (London: Collins, 1976)

—, *Evil and the God of Love* (London: Macmillan, 1977)

—, *God Has Many Names* (London: Macmillan, 1980)

—, *The Second Christianity* (London: SCM, 1983)

—, *Problems of Religious Pluralism* (London: Macmillan, 1985)

—, *Faith and Knowledge* (London: Macmillan, 1988^2)

—, *God and the Universe of Faiths* (London: Macmillan, 1988)

—, *An Interpretation of Religion* (London: Macmillan, 1989)

—, 'A Response to Gerard Loughlin', *Modern Theology* 7 (1990), 57–66

—, *Philosophy of Religion* (London: Prentice-Hall, 1990)

—, 'Rational Theistic Belief without Proofs' in Paul Badham (ed.), *A John Hick Reader* (London: Macmillan, 1990), 49–60

—, 'Religious Faith as Experiencing-as' in Paul Badham (ed.), *A John Hick Reader* (London: Macmillan, 1990), 34–48

—, *Disputed Questions* (London: Macmillan, 1992)

—, *The Metaphor of God Incarnate* (London: SCM, 1993)

—, 'Readers' Responses', *Themelios* 19/3 (1994), 20–21

—, *The Rainbow of Faiths* (London: SCM, 1995)

—, 'Response to R. Douglas Geivett and W. Gary Phillips', in Dennis L. Ockholm and Timothy R. Phillips (eds.), *Four Views on Salvation in a Pluralistic World* (Grand Rapids: Zondervan, 1996), 246–50

—, 'The Possibility of Religious Pluralism: A Reply to Gavin D'Costa', *Religious Studies* 33/2 (1997), 161–6

—, *The Fifth Dimension* (Oxford: Oneworld, 1999)

—, 'Ineffability', *Religious Studies* 38 (2000), 35–46

Hick, John (ed.), *Truth and Dialogue* (London: Sheldon, 1974)

—, *The Myth of God Incarnate* (London: SCM, 1977)

Horton, John, and Susan Mendus (eds.), *After MacIntyre* (Cambridge: Polity, 1994)

Hughes, Dewi Arwel, *Has God Many Names?* (Leicester: Apollos, 1996)

Hume, David, *A Treatise of Human Nature* (Oxford: OUP, 2000)

Insole, Christopher J., 'Why John Hick Cannot, and Should Not, Stay out of the Jam Pot', *Religious Studies* 38 (2000), 25–33

Jaspers, Karl, *The Origin and Goal of History* (tr. Michael Bullock; London: Routledge, 1953)

Johnson, Mark, *Moral Imagination* (London: University of Chicago Press, 1993)

Kamitsuka, David G., 'The Justification of Religious Belief in the Pluralist Public Realm: Another Look at Postliberal Apologetics', *Journal of Religion* 76 (1996), 588–606

Kant, Immanuel, *Religion Within the Limits of Reason Alone* (tr. Theodore M. Greene and Hoyt H. Hudson: New York: Harper & Row, 1960)

—, *On History* (New York: Library of Liberal Arts, 1963)

—, *Prolegomena* (tr. Paul Carus; Illinois: Open Court, 1989)

—, *Critique of Pure Reason* (tr. and eds. Paul Guyer and Allen W. Wood; Cambridge: CUP, 1998)

Kelly, Douglas F., *The Emergence of Liberty in the Modern World* (New Jersey: Presbyterian & Reformed, 1992)

Kemp Smith, Norman, *The Philosophy of David Hume* (London: Macmillan, 1941)

Knitter, Paul F., 'Responsibilities for the Future: Toward an Interfaith Ethic' in John D'Arcy May (ed.), *Pluralism and the Religions* (London: Cassell, 1998)

Kraemer, Hendrick, *Religion and the Christian Faith* (London: Lutterworth, 1956)

Kuhn, Thomas S., *The Structure of Scientific Revolutions* (London: University of Chicago Press, 1970)

Küng, Hans, *Does God Exist?* (London: SCM, 1991)

Küng, Hans, and Karl-Josef Kuschel, *A Global Ethic* (London: SCM, 1993)

Lindbeck, George, *The Nature of Doctrine* (London: SPCK, 1984)

Lipner, Julius J., 'Does Copernicus Help? Reflections for a Christian Theology of Religions', *Religious Studies* 13 (1977), 243–58

Locke, John, *An Essay Concerning Human Understanding* (London: Everyman, 1976)

Loughlin, Gerard, 'Noumenon and Phenomena', *Religious Studies* 23 (1987), 493–508

—, 'Prefacing Pluralism: John Hick and the Mastery of Religion', *Modern Theology* 7 (1990), 29–55

MacIntyre, Alasdair, *Whose Justice? Which Rationality?* (London: Duckworth, 1988)

—, *Three Rival Versions of Moral Enquiry* (London: Duckworth, 1990)

Markham, Ian S., *Plurality and Christian Ethics* (Cambridge: CUP, 1994)

Marshall, I. Howard, 'Myth' in Sinclair B. Ferguson and David F. Wright (eds.), *New Dictionary of Theology* (Leicester: IVP, 1989), 449–451

Mase, Emi, 'Does Hick's Post-Copernican Pluralism in *An Interpretation of Religion* lead to Agnosticism?' (unpublished MA thesis, University of Bristol, 1994)

Mathis, T., *Against John Hick* (Boston: University Press of America, 1985)

McGrath, Alister E., *The Genesis of Doctrine* (Grand Rapids: Eerdmans, 1997)

McMylor, Peter, *Alasdair MacIntyre: Critic of Modernity* (London, Routledge, 1994)

Michalson, Gordon E., *Kant and the Problem of God* (Oxford: Blackwell, 1999)

Middleton, J. Richard, and Brian J. Wash, *Truth Is Stranger than it Used to Be* (London: SPCK, 1995)

Moule, C.F.D., *The Origin of Christology* (Cambridge: CUP, 1978)

Narchison, J. Rosario, 'Theological Education for Pluralism in India' in John D'Arcy May (ed.), *Pluralism and the Religions* (London: Cassell, 1998)

Netland, Harold, *Dissonant Voices* (Leicester: IVP, 1991)

Newbigin, Lesslie, *The Gospel in a Pluralist Society* (London: SPCK, 1989)

—, 'Religion for the Marketplace' in Gavin D'Costa (ed.), *Christian Uniqueness Reconsidered* (New York: Orbis, 1990)

Ogden, Schubert M., 'Problems in the Case for a Pluralistic Theology of Religions', *Journal of Religion* 69 (1988), 493–507

Otto, Rudolf, *The Idea of the Holy* (London: OUP, 1950)

Panikkar, Raimon, *The Intra-Religious Dialogue* (New Jersey: Paulist, 1999)

Pannenberg, Wolfhart, 'Religious Pluralism and Conflicting Truth Claims' in Gavin D'Costa (ed.), *Christian Uniqueness Reconsidered* (New York: Orbis, 1990)

Penelhum, Terence, *God and Skepticism* (Netherlands: D. Reidel, 1983)

—, 'Reflections on the Ambiguity of the World' in Arvind Sharma (ed.), *God, Truth and Reality: Essays in Honour of John Hick* (London: Macmillan, 1993)

Pinnock, Clark, *A Wideness in God's Mercy* (Grand Rapids: Zondervan, 1992)

Plantinga, Alvin (ed.), *The Ontological Argument* (London: Macmillan, 1968)

Plantinga, Alvin, and Nicholas Wolterstorff (eds.), *Faith and Rationality* (Notre Dame: University of Notre Dame Press, 1983)

Race, Alan, *Christians and Religious Pluralism* (London: SCM, 1993²)

Ramachandra, Vinoth, *The Recovery of Mission* (Carlisle: Paternoster, 1996)

—, *Faiths in Conflict?* (Leicester: IVP, 1999)

Rescher, Nicholas, *Kant and the Reach of Reason* (Cambridge: CUP, 2000)

Rowe, William L., 'John Hick's Contribution to the Philosophy of Religion' in Arvind Sharma (ed.), *God, Truth and Reality: Essays in Honour of John Hick* (London: Macmillan, 1993)

Runzo, Joseph, *World-Views and Perceiving God* (London: Macmillan, 1993)

Russell, Bertrand, *Why I Am Not a Christian* (London: George Allen & Unwin, 1975)

—, *A History of Western Philosophy* (London: George Allen & Unwin, 1984)

Sacks, Oliver, *The Man who Mistook his Wife for a Hat* (London: Picador, 1986)

Sanders, John, *No Other Name* (Grand Rapids: Eerdmans, 1992)

Sanders, John (ed.), *What about Those who Have Never Heard?* (Downers Grove: IVP, 1995)

Schleiermacher, Friedrich, *The Christian Faith* (Edinburgh: T. & T. Clark, 1960)

Schrader, George, 'The Thing in Itself in Kantian Philosophy' in Paul Wolff (ed.), *Kant: A Collection of Critical Essays* (London: University of Notre Dame Press, 1968)

Sinkinson, Christopher, 'Scripture and scriptures: The Problem of Hermeneutics in Inter-religious Understanding', *Discernment* 2 (1994), 12–23

—, *John Hick: An Introduction to his Theology* (Leicester: RTSF, 1995)

—, 'Is Christianity Better than Other Religions?' *Expository Times* 107/9 (1996), 260–65

—, 'Confessing Christ in a Pluralist Culture' in Timothy Bradshaw (ed.), *Grace and Truth in the Secular Age* (Cambridge: Eerdmans, 1998)

— 'In Defence of the Faith: Clark Pinnock and the World Religions' in Tony Gray and Christopher Sinkinson (eds.), *Reconstructing Theology* (Carlisle: Paternoster, 2000)

Smith, Wilfred Cantwell, *The Meaning and End of Religion* (Minneapolis: Fortress, 1991)

—, *Patterns of Faith Around the World* (Oxford: Oneworld, 1998)

Soskice, Janet Martin, *Metaphor and Religious Language* (Oxford: Clarendon, 1988)

Sullivan, Francis A., *Salvation Outside the Church?* (London: Geoffrey Chapman, 1992)

Swinburne, Richard, *The Existence of God* (Oxford: OUP, 1979)

—, *Faith and Reason* (Oxford: Clarendon, 1983)

Verduin, Leonard, *The Reformers and their Stepchildren* (Grand Rapids: Eerdmans, 1964)

Ward, Keith, *A Vision to Pursue* (London: SCM, 1991)

—, *Religion and Revelation* (Oxford: Clarendon, 1994)

Westphal, Merold, 'In Defence of the Thing in Itself', *Kant-Studien* (1968), 118–41

Williams, Stephen, 'The Trinity and "Other Religions"' in Kevin J. Vanhoozer (ed.), *The Trinity in a Pluralistic Age* (Grand Rapids: Eerdmans, 1997)

Willis, Geoffrey Grimshaw, *Saint Augustine and the Donatist Controversy* (London: SPCK, 1950)

Wittgenstein, Ludwig, *Philosophical Investigations* (Oxford: Blackwell, 1967)

Wright, Nigel Goring, *Disavowing Constantine: Mission, Church and the Social Order in the Theologies of John Howard Yoder and Jürgen Moltmann* (Carlisle: Paternoster, 2000)